THE PORNOGRAPHIC AGE

THE PORNOGRAPHIC AGE

ALAIN BADIOU

Translated, edited and with an Afterword by
A. J. Bartlett and Justin Clemens

Commentary by William Watkin

BLOOMSBURY ACADEMIC
LONDON • NEW YORK • OXFORD • NEW DELHI • SYDNEY

BLOOMSBURY ACADEMIC
Bloomsbury Publishing Plc
50 Bedford Square, London, WC1B 3DP, UK
1385 Broadway, New York, NY 10018, USA

BLOOMSBURY, BLOOMSBURY ACADEMIC and the Diana logo are
trademarks of Bloomsbury Publishing Plc

First published in 2013 in France as 'Pornographie du temps present' by
Alain Badiou
© Librairie Arthème Fayard

First published in Great Britain 2020

Design by Irene Martinez Costa
Cover image: *Masks and Death* by James Ensor (1860–1949)
Musee d'Art Moderne et d'Art Contemporain, Liege, Belgium/
Bridgeman Images © DACS 2017

A catalogue record for this book is available from the British Library.

A catalog record for this book is available from the Library of Congress.

ISBN: HB: 978-1-3500-1478-7
        PB: 978-1-3500-1479-4
        ePDF: 978-1-3500-1477-0
        eBook: 978-1-3500-1480-0

Typeset by RefineCatch Limited, Bungay, Suffolk

To find out more about our authors and books visit www.bloomsbury.com
and sign up for our newsletters.

CONTENTS

EDITOR'S NOTE

This text is a reworked version of the conference presentation 'Images of the Present Time', given by Alain Badiou in the great amphitheatre of the Sorbonne, 26 January 2013, for the Philosophy Forum *France Culture*.

ACKNOWLEDGEMENTS

Aside from Alain Badiou himself, the translators would like to thank Lia Hills, Helen Johnson and Angela Cullip for their indispensable aid with the preparation of this translation. At Bloomsbury, Liza Thompson and Frankie Mace.

The Pornographic Age

Alain Badiou

Philosophy easily becomes a nostalgic exercise. Moreover, contemporary philosophy tends to flaunt this nostalgia. It almost always declares that something is forgotten, erased, absent. Philosophers often imagine that they have invented this melancholy cult of the loss of everything of value and, finally, the loss of the present itself; but the poets have said in melancholy there is no longer a sense, no longer a feeling, for the liveliness of the present. 'A present is lacking' is Mallarmé's formula.[1] And Rimbaud: 'we are not in this world'.[2] This means: contemporaneity itself is lacking. As if, between our thought and the present world, there were a gap, very old, long identified by philosophy, but perhaps increasing today. Or perhaps more difficult to identify.

I would like to attempt to show this gap, to take the risk, if not of the present, at least of what separates us from it, and which is of the order of representation, the order of the image. In short, to repeat the ancient attempt to produce a real analysis of the images of the present age. Or at least to undertake a kind of description of the regime of images, in so far as they deliver us the times – or, rather, don't deliver them.

As often, my guide will be something non-philosophical, a piece of theatre, Jean Genet's *The Balcony*.[3]

The subject of this play, *The Balcony*, is precisely what is at stake in an expression such as 'images of the present age'. In fact, Genet's text asks explicitly what becomes of images when the present is disorder. For Genet, it is that of riots or revolution; for us, it is undoubtedly the Arab Spring, the movement of the Indignados, at the same time as that of the crisis of capitalism and its deleterious effects in Europe.

Genet works therefore on the relation between images and the uncertainty – even the invisibility – of the present.

Jacques Lacan has dedicated a long analysis to Genet's play.[4] Like Freud, who found a whole part of his theory in the plays of Sophocles, Lacan knew that the theatre is a major resource when it comes to understanding the mechanism which transforms the real into representation and desire into images, when it is a matter of extorting through imaginary manoeuvres subjects' consent to the power that separates them from their own creative capacities. In this way, he insists on a point of formal appearance. He considers it essential to understand that *The Balcony* is a comedy.

He defines comedy in this way: 'Comedy embraces, gathers and takes enjoyment from the relationship with an effect ... namely the appearance of this signified called the phallus.'[5] The most important word here is 'appearing' [*apparition*]. Tragedy is the majestic melancholy of destiny: it says that the Truth is in the past. Comedy is always, on the contrary, a comedy of the present, because it makes the phallus appear, that is to say, the authentic symbol of this present. The theatre alone points out the comical appearance of what power is in the present, and thus opens it to derision. In every tragedy, we see the dark melancholy of power. In every comedy, we see the farcical semblant.

One can therefore say that my goal – and this is one of the primary senses of the word 'image' – is to find the register of the *philosophical* comedy of the present, by naming, if you'll permit me the expression, the speculative Phallus of our present.

The power [*puissance*] of comedy is to show that, beneath its pompous emblems, naked power [*pouvoir*] cannot dissimulate its ferocity or its emptiness forever.

What names are put into play in the philosophical comedy of the present, of our present? What are today's pompous emblems of power? What is its untouchable value? How is it that there is an unfortunate presence of the present? To my eyes, the principal name is 'democracy'.[6]

To avoid any misunderstanding, let us agree that the word 'democracy' does not cover any theory, or fiction, of a shared power of the *demos*, of an effective sovereignty of the people. It will only be a question of the word 'democracy' in so far as it designates a form of the State and all that goes with it. It is a constitutional category, a juridical hypostasis. It is the form of public liberties, supposedly protected by the constitution and animated by the electoral process. It is the form of the 'Rule of Law' [*l'État de droit*], to which all the so-called Western powers lay claim, as those countries that live in the shelter of those powers try to do, or, as their clients, pretend to agree to.

It is clear that, even in this restricted definition, the word 'democracy' is supposed to capture all hearts, and it is to this name that a universal hymn of praise is raised. Representative democracy and its constitutional organization obviously provide what is today incontrovertible of our political life. It is our fetish.

To make the comedy of images exist today is thus, almost inevitably, to treat the name 'democracy' for what it is: the Phallus of our present. To win, beyond the monotonous presence of our everyday life, the life of a true present, requires the courage to go beyond the democratic fetish as we know it. Jean Genet's *The Balcony* can serve as the preliminary operator.

The Balcony confronts the reign of images with the real of revolt. We start from a figure of order as the order of images, namely a brothel. The brothel is the exemplary figure of something rigidly ordered – it is under the implacable control of a character named Irma – something closed on its law, but which, at the same time, is governed entirely by the imaginary. Genet sees, in the 1950s, that which is absolutely visible today: what reveals the hidden ferocity of power is the proliferation of the obscenity of images, which is to say the fusion, at all levels, including the cultural and political, of the potentially sophisticated arousal of a desire with the vulgarity of commercial propaganda. The brothel is the theatrical place of this fusion: that which presents there as the object of desire, in costume and adorned, is immediately convertible into cash. The brothel is the place where the average price of desire is evaluated and fixed. It is the market of images.

Outside, however, the workers' revolt grinds on, as it grinds on today, mostly outside the Western brothel, among the mine-workers of South Africa, in the thousands of worker revolts in China, or also at the birth of the Arab Spring. But also, for us, in the youth abandoned at the periphery of our major towns, or in the *foyers* where African workers are crammed together.

This outside of the brothel presents the figure of the real, the figure of life. It is the pure present, either as a fit of rage or as infinite patience.

The whole problem is to know what the relation or non-relation is between the pure evental exteriority and the field of images, where the latent power of the event, the as-yet unrevealed sense of revolt, almost always comes to be lost in a representation without thought. The problem is as much the relation or non-relation between the patience of the real and the impatient excitation that images attempt to impose, in order that everyone might resolve to pass, without any links, in this incoherence of impatience, from one thing to another, as one passes from one model of car to another. The play's question is that of the existence or the absence of a desire, which, as Lacan said, would not be a semblant. A desire animated by the real and not by images.

What is it about this desire that makes it a problem? Well, politically, it is a desire for revolution, which would bring about the real equality of all humanity; in poetry, a sublime desire, by which a particular language, worked in its depths, rises to a level of universal clarity; in mathematics, a desire for intellectual beatitude, which alone procures the certainty of having resolved an extremely difficult problem and offering its solution to all; in love, a desire that the experience of life, in all its domains, be more intense and precise as two than when alone.[7] Such are the desires that, to touch on their real, must clear themselves of numerous images. Philosophy summarizes them all in stating that every authentic desire concerns the absoluteness of its object.

But can there be such an absolute desire – a desire for art, politics, science or love – which is not a fantasmatic desire? The profound question of *The Balcony*, posed more particularly to the political real, thus to that which in its time is called revolution, is the following: can we subtract ourselves from images?

In the foreword to the play, Genet writes:

Some poets, in our day, are engaged in a very curious operation: they sing the People, Liberty, the Revolution, etc., which, being sung, are thrown and then nailed to an abstract sky where they figure, discomfited and deflated, in deformed constellations. Disembodied, they become untouchable. How to approach them, love them, live them, if they are dispatched so magnificently far off? Writings, sometimes lavishly, become the constitutive signs of a poem, the poetry being nostalgia and the song destroying its pretext, our poets kill what they would like to make live.[8]

In short, the difficulty is that the relation between the real and images – in the play, the insurrection at the brothel – is dramatically contradictory. For as soon as it is captured by the image, seized by the nostalgia of a fantasmatic desire, the real is crucified, abolished. The image is the murder of the pure present. In the play, as we'll see, the person who engineers this murder is the Chief of Police.

The result is that, for us, any advance within the images of the present age is largely the attempt to grasp what has no image. The present of the present has no image. We must disimage, disimagine.[9]

The difficulty is that naked power, which hides behind the subtle plasticity and seductive obscenity of the images of the democratic and commercial world, does not itself have an image; it is well and truly naked, but this, far from delivering us from images, ensures their power. The real of power is certainly a power of the present, but is not, as such, subjected to the images of this present: it is what is hidden behind contemporary democratic imagery.

The character in Genet's play who shows on stage this power without image of the image is, as you'd expect, the Police Chief.

Every situation, the theatre tells us, has its Police Chief, who is the un-seductive emblem of the power [*puissance*] with which naked power [*pouvoir*] animates seductive images.

The drama of the Police Chief, in Genet's play, is that nobody desires this character, no-one comes into the brothel to enjoy themselves by dressing as the Chief of Police. He is the emblem of naked power, because he is left out of the account of images, contrary to the great sportsman, television presenter, professional benefactor, top model, state president, or show-business billionaire, who are its profiteers.

Such is, in Lacan's eyes, the proof that he is indeed the phallus. And, in effect, toward the end of the play, the Police Chief, desperately seeking a desirable gala dress, announces that it has been suggested to him that he dress up as a 'prick of great stature', which also means: as an absolute image of the commercial desire of the brothel's clients.

We are at the end of the goings on. The insurrection is out of breath, and the proletarian leader declares: 'Outside, in what you call life, everything has crashed. No truth was possible.'[10] Which shows that, outside of the image is not only the real, but the real as truth. A great philosophical teaching, said in passing. The outside of the commodity and its universe is not only the real of production or circulation, but above all the creation of a political truth.

In Genet's play, this political truth is lacking, and the entire exterior real fades to images.

It is at this moment that the Chief finds his costume. Observe this amazing scene:

The Envoy (*ironically*) No, nobody's come yet. Nobody has yet felt the need to abolish himself in your fascinating image.

The Chief of Police That means the projects you submitted to me aren't very effective. (To the Queen) Nothing? Nobody?

The Queen (*very gently*) Nobody. And yet, the blinds have been drawn again. The men ought to be coming in. Besides, the apparatus has been set up; so we'll be informed by a full peal of bells.

. . . .

The Chief of Police I like my image to be at once legendary and humane.[11] That it participate undoubtedly in eternal principles, but so you recognize my mug.... The latest image that was proposed to me ... I hardly dare mention it to you.

The Judge Was it ... very audacious?

The Chief of Police Very. Too audacious. I'd never dare tell you what it was. (Suddenly, he seems to make up his mind.) Gentlemen, I have sufficient confidence in your judgment and devotion. After all, I want to carry on the fight by boldness of ideas as well. It was this: I've been advised to appear in the form of a gigantic phallus, a prick of great stature ...

(*The Three Figures and the Queen are dumbfounded.*)

The Queen George! You?

The Chief of Police What do you expect? If I'm to symbolize the nation, your joint ...

The Envoy (*to the Queen*) Allow him, Madame. It's the tone of the age.

The Judge A phallus? Of great stature? You mean – enormous?

The Chief of Police Of my stature.

The Judge But that'll be very difficult to bring off.

The Envoy Not so very. What with new techniques and our rubber industry, remarkable things can be worked out. No I'm not worried about that, but rather … (*turning to the Bishop*) … what the Church will think of it?

The Bishop (*after reflection, shrugging his shoulders*) No definite pronouncement can be made this evening. To be sure, the idea is a bold one. (*To the Chief of Police*) But if your case is desperate, we shall have to examine the matter. For … it would be a formidable figurehead, and if you were to transmit yourself in that guise to posterity …

The Queen (*frightened*) No room is provided for, no salon is equipped. … And finally my house is esteemed for its imagination, but also for its modesty and high tone.

The Chief of Police Would you like to see the model?[12]

We see, in this penultimate comedic turn of the play, when the naked power of the police shows itself as phallus, that we have the assembling of a structure. It's this structure that we can use to decipher the present age. And the fidelity to living Marxism is then the fidelity to what Marx first put at the centre of any construction of a political truth: what he named ideology, and whose relation of imagery to the real was what had to be undone to create an active consciousness of class struggle.

Let's summarize the structure assembled by Genet. There are four terms:

The brothel, as the place of the legislation of images, the *jouissance* of simulacra.

The exterior, where the precarity of the real insurrection is announced.

The Police Chief, who embodies the power of which images are the operators.

The ultimate emblem: the phallus, the image of that which has no image, naked power.

This combinatorics orients us in posing four questions to the present age:

1   What is the imaginary cover of the present? What exactly is our brothel, its commercial authority [*instance*] and/or its political pornography? Let's call this moment that of systematic analysis.

2   What are the real outlines of what subtracts itself from the image? Are political truths, subtracted from images, possible? Disimaging, disimagining – is it possible? This methodical stage is that of the exception. Let's call it: political experience.

3   What, in the testing of truths, which we suppose possible, guards the facticity of the present? What is the name of

naked power, anonymous power? What is the obscure and invisible guarantor of power? This time, it is a matter of the designation of naked power and separating from it, violently if necessary. This methodical stage is that of disjunction.

4 What is the emblem of naked power? What is the phallus of the present age? This methodical stage is that of poetic analysis.

Thus the four operations for seeing clearly from the balcony of the present are: a systematic operation, a political operation, a disjunctive operation and a poetic operation.

The most serious problem, the most difficult, is to find an order that links the four operations, that is fitted to the present. When we have found this order, we can define a rigorous method of investigation of the present age. I have no intention here of finding this order. I will say only that we must begin with the fourth operation, the poetic operation, the one with which to think the emblem of the present age. It is necessary to pose the question: what is the phallic fetish of our age? It is, as I have already noted, something we can and should answer without hesitation: the emblem of the present age, its fetish, which covers with a false image naked power without image, is the word 'democracy', such as I have fixed its precise and limited definition. Today, it is a sentimental obligation to be a democrat. The ferocious naked power which destroys us is recognized and even loved by all when it is covered by the word 'democracy'; just as the Chief of Police hopes for the desire of all when he appears dressed as a prick. We must above all treat methodically this obligation and this love. We must remove democratic sentimentality from our souls. If not, the conclusion will be very bleak – the present will sooner or later fall into the worst.

Genet's conclusion, let's note in passing, is precisely very bitter. For two reasons. Firstly, it is that the triumph of images is complete. Indeed, and this is the final comedic turn, a client turns up at the door of the brothel whose desire for enjoyment is to be identified as the Chief of Police, a hitherto unknown desire. And who is this client? Roger, the leader of the proletarian insurrection.

Genet's is a powerful meditation upon the ending up of revolutions in the police tomb that is the power of the state. What the revolutionary succumbs to is the image of naked power. The second of Genet's bitter poetics is that the play itself seems circular, as if nothing, except the tomb of the dream, could happen. At the very end of *The Balcony*, Irma, who played the role of the Queen during the insurrection, becomes Irma again, the Madame [*patronne*] of the brothel. We hear a submachine gun, the final burst of the exterior real, and Madame Irma asks: Who's that? Is it a rebel, is it an agent of power? It is, says the Envoy – a Machiavellian agent of repression and the Chief of

Police's handyman – 'someone dreaming'. Then Irma turns out the lights and everything ends with a beautiful monologue:

> It took so much light . . . a thousand francs worth of electricity a day! Thirty-eight studios! Every one of them gilded, and all of them rigged with machinery so as to be able to fit into and combine with each other . . . And all these performances so that I can remain alone, mistress and assistant mistress of this house and of myself. (She pushes in a button, then pushes it out again.) Oh no, that's the tomb. He needs light, for two thousand years! . . . and food for two thousand years . . . (She shrugs her shoulders.) Oh well, everything's in working order, and dishes have been prepared. Glory means descending into the grave with tons of victuals! . . . (She calls out, facing the wings:) Carmen? Carmen? . . . Bolt the doors, my dear, and put the furniture-covers on . . . (She continues extinguishing.) In a little while, I'll have to start all over again . . . put all the lights on again . . . dress up . . . (A cock crows.) Dress up . . . ah, the disguises! Distribute roles again . . . assume my own . . . (She stops in the middle of the stage, facing the audience.) . . . Prepare yours . . . judges, generals, bishops, chamberlains, rebels who allow the revolt to congeal, I'm going to prepare my costumes and studios for tomorrow. . . . You must now go home, where everything – you can be quite sure – will be falser than here. . . . You must go now. You'll leave by the right,

through the alley … (She extinguishes the last light.) It's morning already. (A burst of machine-gun fire.)[13]

Here, Genet's thesis is evidently that the momentary image is only thinkable as return, a return of representations of which the theatre is the least false figure (elsewhere, Genet says, everything is more false still). The only eternity is circularity. Desire is only ever the resumption of power, but power presented as image. We see here a variant on Nietzsche's thesis, on the nihilistic coupling between affirmation and circularity. Even the sound of the machine gun only indicates the eternal return of a defeated action.

The key problem, for anyone who wants to escape the power of power, is to disengage from one's enchainment to images, and for that to know the Police Chief by his most intimate convictions. What is the subjective motivation for consenting to the world as it goes?

Since the idea of revolution has disappeared, our world is merely that of the resumption of power, under the consensual and pornographic image of market democracy.

My optimism is that a strong, organized and popular thought, which would face up to this resumption, can interrupt the cycle of return which has brought us back to this state of things – the undisputed domination of the spirit of unfettered capitalism – similar to that of the 1840s.

But with one condition: we must understand, and this is very difficult for us, that the true critique of the world, today, is not to return to the academic critique of the capitalist economy. Nothing is more facile, nothing is more abstract, nothing is more useless than the critique of capitalism reduced to itself. Those who make the most noise over this critique inevitably come to propose some sage reforms to capitalism. They propose a regulated and decent capitalism, a non-pornographic capitalism, an ecological capitalism, and always more democracy. They demand, in short, a comfortable capitalism for all: a capitalism with a human face. Nothing will emerge from these chimeras.

The only dangerous and radical critique is the political critique of democracy. Because the emblem of the present age, its fetish, its phallus, is democracy. So long as we do not know how to construct a large-scale creative critique of State democracy, we will remain, stagnate, in the financial brothel of images. We will be in the service of the couple formed by the Madame of the brothel and the Chief of Police: the couple of consumable images and naked power.

At the moment, we are between two worlds. We all know, I think, that our age is an intervallic 'today'. 'Democracy' too is an intervallic word, a word that does not know where it came from, nor where it is going, nor even what it means. A word which merely covers our passive desire for comfort, the satisfaction with our intellectual misery, captured in the term 'middle class'.

I recently read an article by a Russian opponent of Putin. He, like all the press, praised what he saw as the emergence in Russia and China of a new middle class, which he declared the bearer of democratic ideology. He praised this ideology in two respects, constitutional and resistant. The middle class, he said, aspires to genuine elections, honest, not rigged; but it is also capable of courageously marching in the streets and opposing Putin's police. The middle class appears as an established base of constitutional regularity and liberal protest. If this democratic price is paid, there will be only academic and reformist inconveniences for the formidable capitalist machine, the real of naked power.

But what is this 'middle class'? Our Russian opponent defines it in a fashion as comical as it is veridical. Of this democratic middle class, he says: 'It consumes and it is connected.' The hardcore consumer of digital information, such is the democrat who confronts Putin.

We recognize here, very clearly, the democratic imagery, at the same time as the risible misrecognition of the Chief of Police mindset which ordains its adoration and imitation. It is in this middling subjectivity, whose ideal is to persevere in its being, that its mass support, its class support, resides the world over, and especially in the Western world, in the State called democratic; even if, by the Rule of Law [*État de droit*], by the State whose famous 'Western values' order its right to military intervention anywhere that there are succulent raw materials, we see, day after day, that this kind of State is, in a properly stupefying fashion, the base of the power of capital.

Make no mistake about it: beyond the archaic despotism of Putin, our Russian opponent visibly aspires in all his being to just such a State. It is that the middle-class individual, which we all partially are, desires to persevere in the world as it is, provided that capitalism proposes it a less despotic, more consensual authority, and a better regulated corruption in which it can participate without even having to take account of it. This is perhaps the best definition of the contemporary middle class: to participate naïvely in the formidable inegalitarian corruption of capitalism, without even having to know it. Others, a very small number, higher up, will know it for them.

Such is truly the contemporary state of things: the middle class revels in teleported goods and images, whereas the revolution, communism, much like dead stars, gravitate away, deprived of any affirmative image and mired in imagery where the dominant world and its army of Police Chiefs imagine they can contain them forever.

In a youthful piece, *Emperor and Galilean*, Ibsen traces the history of Julian the Apostate, so called because he wanted to restore paganism after Constantine, after the conversion of the Empire to Christianity.[14] According to Ibsen, Julian the Apostate, balanced between the aesthetic inheritance of the Greeks and the Christian revelation, magnificently declares: 'The old beauty is no longer beautiful and the new truth is not yet true.'[15] What is the present age – for we others – who are trying to keep open the door by which one escapes Plato's cave, the democratic reign of images? It is an age in which the old revolutionary politics is no longer active, and where the new politics is, with difficulty, experimenting with its truth. We are the experimenters of the interval. We are between two worlds, one of which is falling little by little into oblivion, and the other is only fragmentary. It's a matter of passing [*passer*]. We are smugglers [*passeurs*]. We create from fragments a politics without fetishes, not even, above all not, the democratic fetish. As one of the rebels says in *The Balcony*:

> How to approach Liberty, the People, Virtue, and how to love
> them if we magnify them? If they are rendered untouchable?
> They must be left in their living reality. We can prepare poems
> and images, not to satisfy but to irritate.[16]

Let us prepare, then, if we know how – but we always know a little – those poems and those images which are not the satisfaction of our enslaved desires. Let us prepare the poetic nudity of the present.

Minus something indefinable

A. J. Bartlett and Justin Clemens

Pornosophical philotheology

JAMES JOYCE, *Ulysses*

This little book first appeared in French in 2013 under the title *Pornographie du temps présent*, literally, *Pornography of the Present Time*. For a number of reasons, not least euphony, we decided to translate the title as *The Pornographic Age* (hereafter simply *Pornography*). This Afterword seeks to situate the book, its procedures and its claims, in some detail because – despite its brevity, accessibility and occasional nature – *Pornography* is simultaneously a dense and thoughtful text, whose preconditions and implications extend far beyond the facts of its immediate presentation.

As translators of several of Badiou's little books and articles, as
commentators on Badiou's writings, and as editors of various
collections of essays on his work, we have previously also been
the authors of a number of such putative texts: introductions,
commentaries, forewords, afterwords and so on.[1] If we ourselves
wonder just how many such 'comments' to Badiou's work anybody
needs, themselves becoming pornographic in the sense discussed
both above *and* below, we mark this relationship from the outset
here in order thereby to emphasize the key problems and
problematics of *transmission*, that is, pedagogy, itself a central
consideration for Badiou's philosophy. In *Pornography*, this
problematic of transmission-pedagogy bears integrally upon the
question of the construction, circulation and consequences of
images today – that is, upon their *pornographic* nature.

Hence the book's title. It asserts an essential connection
between 'pornography' and the 'times', the 'age', in which we live.
'Pornography' is a genre that is often held to flourish in, if not
exemplify, our age. One can even be surprised at the number and
eminence of philosophers and critics for whom pornography
has proven a central category for thought, bearing upon the
aesthetics and politics of images, stages, gazes, not to mention
time itself.[2] Yet its limits and conventions can seem, even beyond
the intense controversies that the term constitutively inspires,
complex and confused. As Ian Hunter, David Saunders and
Dugald Williamson have put it, 'pornography' generally functions

as a 'circumstantial' designation rather than a well-defined category, variously designating 'an eroticising device, a target of medical and pedagogical programmes, a tradable commodity, an aesthetic category, an object of feminist and governmental reforms, [and] a legal problem'.[3] This is certainly correct, but it is *also* the case that a certain historical and conceptual consistency characterizes the word. As Lynn Hunt notes:

> The word *pornography* appeared for the first time in the *Oxford English Dictionary* in 1857, and most of the English variations on the word (*pornographer* and *pornographic*) date from the middle or the end of the nineteenth century. The words emerged in French a little sooner. According to the *Trésor de la langue française*, *pornographe* surfaced first in Restif de la Bretonne's treatise of 1769 titled *Le Pornographe* to refer to writing about prostitution, and *pornographique*, *pornographe* and *pornographie* in the sense of obscene writing or images dated from the 1830s and 1840s.[4]

Moreover, as Hunt adds, 'Significantly, it was only in the decades of the emergence of mass politics – the 1880s and afterward – that most countries began to produce their own indigenous pornography, a fact again suggestive of the link between pornography and democracy.'[5] We would especially like to underline the historical bond that Hunt discerns here between 'pornography' and 'democracy', for it is one that Badiou too confirms, if here at the level of the concept rather than at the level of history, and with rather different ends in mind.

A well-known deadlock of what we now call 'neo-liberalism' – that is, the contemporary total economization of the cult of individual freedoms – is that the absolute primacy given to individual choice occludes structural oppressions, but attempting to counter such individualism by focusing on structural oppression occludes the potential for a universalism irreducible to an endless warfare of identities. This is part of the logic by which 'democracy' has become the dominant political watchword or symptom of our age. Moreover, it is bound up with how 'pornography' has become the dominant genre: pornography incites the uptake of new technologies as it moves from being a marginal to a billion-dollar industry by enforcing an absolute prohibition on the prohibition of images. Nothing, including this book, subject as it has been by the publishers to the essentially pornographic circulation of identities and markets, is allowed to escape being represented; but, in the ferocious turbulence of representations, the crucial difference between representations and the real is effaced. 'So,' as Julian Murphet writes, 'while capitalism continues to thrive on the basis of a progressive rise in the degree of rationalization, it offsets that with an obscenely irrational compulsion to enjoy, a collective self-sacrificial ritual of unfulfillable pleasure at the altar of a ubiquitous pornography'.[6] In this sense, then, the pornographic is not primarily the imagistic, graphic or embodied presentation of obscene acts, but a global restructuring of representation that mandates transgression-as-emancipation as a securing of order. Pornography, under such a description, is the agent and guarantor of the privatization of the means of communication as such.

In such a society of the spectacle – 'the present age'! – is it still possible to turn the image against itself without simply repeating and extending its pornographic logic? If so, how? With what means? It is at this point that Badiou has recourse to the theatre, more particularly to a famous play by Jean Genet, *The Balcony*. If such a recourse, and the justifications for such a recourse, are of inherent philosophical interest, we should not overlook the ideological difficulties that this might cause Badiou in particular. If we can always ask 'what is the role of the theatre in politics?' and 'what is the role of theatre for philosophy?', the further issue here is this: how can a Platonist speak in praise of the theatre, when it is precisely theatre, its images, and the unconstrained affects that it supposedly licenses, that must be excluded from the Republic in the name of justice? Is not theatre finally in systematic solidarity with the pornography of the contemporary world? Is Badiou not risking performative contradiction with this reliance? Of course, one thing that Badiou does not do here is rely on the facile, contemporary conception of Platonism as authoritarian, joyless and frigid. Such a Platonism, ubiquitous in the schools, is itself a condition of our pornographic age.

Badiou's engagement with the theatre is a lifelong commitment. Typically, as he recounts in the long interview with Nicholas Truong, it begins in an encounter. 'The first theatrical production that really struck me I encountered in Toulouse when I was 14. *La Compagnie du Grenier* [The Attic Company], founded by Maurice Sarrazin, was putting on "Scapin the Schemer".'[7] Scapin is a character who will remain with Badiou. In one of his own plays, Badiou rewrites him as Ahmed the Philosopher[8] and, according to Oliver Feltham, Badiou himself operates as Scapin, a man who, subject to diverse conditions, 'creates as he finds his own milieu'.[9] As Badiou tells it, this early encounter with Scapin, with Daniel Sorano's performance of it, coupled with his own later performances of the character – critically praised, he notes, for recalling the Sorano original – will have seen him catch 'the theatre bug'.[10] But this is only concretized for him in an act of thought. He recounts the performance of Vilar in another of Molière's plays, *Don Juan*: 'the character was demonstrating his uncertainty, engaging in a tense examination of various hypotheses one could make in relation to an abnormal situation. Yes, this art of hypotheses, of possibilities, this *trembling of thought before the inexplicable* – this was the theatre in its highest expression' (emphasis added).[11]

We need not labour the point of the history of Badiou's engagement with the theatre as player, writer, spectator, critic or even theorist, and indeed it seems apropos to note what he says in his extended work on the subject, *Rhapsody for the Theatre*, wherein the established complicity of theatre and the state is at stake. Speaking of François Regnault – 'a man destined to theatre' – and his work *The Spectator*, Badiou says: 'His guide would give us a different outlook from mine: the outlook of the man of the theatre, which is what Regnault is and which I am not.'[12] What matters in terms of situating this text, *The Pornographic Age*, is to consider the terms of the impossibility of the relation between philosophy and theatre (and ultimately the not-impossible distinction between Theatre and State thereby) and precisely because, as he himself says in this text, concerned as it is with the domination of images, '[A]s often, my guide will be something non-philosophical, a piece of theatre . . .'.[13] A piece of Theatre in order to *see* the contemporary state (of the situation).

We say the 'impossibility' of this relation precisely because Badiou the philosopher, as a Platonist, self-declared at least since 1988's *Manifesto for Philosophy*,[14] seems for these reasons to have set himself up with a real problem: that of rendering thinkable this very (non)relation, given philosophy founds itself on its subtraction from the poetics of theatre, from theatre's predominant place in terms of the transmission of knowledge and, thus, finally, in terms of what knowledge is for an age or an epoch. Badiou's atypical Platonism, to which we will return below, realizes an atypical question. Not: 'how to have done with the theatre from the position of "philosophy"?', but: 'how can the knowledge of images, which is the theatre, help us subtract ourselves from the knowledge of images?' This is to say that, for Badiou, for whom theatre is not, ultimately, an enemy of thought but one of its necessary conditions, *how can the thought of theatre be thought?* As we will see, this is not an aesthetics – always, in one way or another, the bringing of thought *to* theatre – but the means to put *into* thought what Theatre thinks as and for itself, what Theatre and only Theatre can stage and show.

This stake in knowledge that Plato recognizes in theatre, in poetry, in what circulates as knowledge, in terms of what conditions it and of what counts as knowledge, and what knowledge thereby counts to exist, is also a political question. The Greek theatre was a duty and a pedagogy. It put the *polis* on stage, as it were – the forms of its political representation were represented there for all to see, for all to know, for all, in effect, to repeat. But such theatre was also an effect of distance in so far as the figures of this *polis* were, as Badiou says, 'unlikely': 'Theatre, conditioned by democracy, aims at it through a legendary monarchical distance.' Even Genet's *The Balcony* does this, populating the brothel with 'a defunct republic of notables, from a Cross and a Sword that evoke Boulanger rather than Pompidou'. He continues: 'And nobody, it must be said, has ever been able to play or put onstage his solar rebel – to the contrary, the unpunished vice of the text excels in supporting, on the stage, the dickhead of the police prefect.'[15] The theatre, then, in this sense of the nexus of theatre and state, gives us what there is to see of the present –

Genet's brothel is our contemporary; every parliament, itself archaic, is proof of its representation – but it keeps it at arm's length. The 'rebel', the people, the public, as the chance to not be such, are condemned to watch, not participate, given that we are none of these figures of representation – nor can we be![16]

We know that the Republic, the ideal or just city, is founded by Plato on the basis of the impossibility of imitation or representation, the knowledge of the poets, being what counts as knowledge. In other words, to make representation or the knowledge of images impossible is the very condition of possibility for the just city. Hence the theatre of the poets, whether on stage or in the law courts or in the boardroom, as the *pedagogy of representation*.[17] But we should note that Plato's city is, as he says, a city in words, nowhere visible but not impossible. If Socrates, Glaucon, Adeimantas, etc., desire to see these words turned into action, then the distinction between the theatre and the city, the theatre and its state, is itself in question. After all, making words manifest in action is one definition of theatre, and Socrates is without doubt the most singular character of all philosophy, a man of flesh and bone, but who appears in the dialogues as the very figure of what is singularly without representation. In contradistinction with the orators, he is subject to truth.[18]

We might say that, for Plato, every word we use is already divided in two, or, at least, that we usually use words in an equivocal fashion. Moreover, we do this in such a way that we both know and don't know it, even as we do it. Hence the corruption of everyday discourse, which, in so far as it is a corruption, must nonetheless retain a trace of the good, a good which, through philosophy, must be able to be restituted in the name of justice. For even those partisans of the flux who condemn – as is often said these days – 'binary thinking' to the benefit of fluidity, of mixed or amorphous identities, of constantly shifting ensembles of matter-in-performance, necessarily rely upon such thinking to negotiate the self-same supposed flux. We speak as if we knew of what we speak, but we don't; and even though we know we don't know, we refuse to know our own non-knowledge. This gap is what poetry licenses. Into the bargain, poetry claims to be divinely inspired, that is, to be the influx of a god whose sayings cannot be contradicted, if indeed already-inconsistent sayings can be properly contradicted.

Plato, the artist of all this non-art, sets himself up without ambiguity as a rival. The *dia*logues, set as they are in the eternal present, or presented by others outside them as so present, is, precisely, thereby, the *constitution* of a present. We see ordinary characters encounter each other and recount the encounters of the dialogue whose present they enact. Note too that the poets were primarily oral performers, the sophists prose writers; the former inspired, the latter demonstrative. The figure of Socrates is at once a cross between the performer-who-does-not-write and the questioner-in-dialogue, an unprecedented diagonal of encounters. How often these encounters happen in the street should be noted, but what is put into effect here is what Plato calls *participation*.[19] The dialogue is itself a universal address. The rebel is staged in dialogue as the thought of all – but, as noted, such a figure cannot be represented only in thought.

Plato's formalization of what theatre deems impossible – under the condition of the putative mathematics of his time, both conceptually and as prescribed for the training of the philosopher who will not, thereby, be an actor of the ideal but the guardian of its truth – a city in words, addressed to all as participation, is set up in the Republic as the response to his own explicit staging of the problem of the state of theatre in the '*analogy*' of the cave'. Whether 'analogy' is the right word for this *pièce de théâtre*, this image, dedicated to us as the (ir)rational, pedagogical kernel of the *Republic* – as if it organizes structurally the very event within the dialogue that the 'analogy' itself illustrates as central to the possibility of the prisoner's (re) orientation to the truth of the real – might be a matter of conjecture.[20] For what does it actually stand comparison or correspond to? It's a question of education, Plato avers: the knowledge of the city, of the city as itself and for itself. It's a political question that must be seen as such in order to be thought through.

Theatre stages politics as tragedy, as the destiny of great powers, *or* as comedy, the ironical voiding of these same powers. If we felt like providing a diagnosis, we might say that Plato stages in the Cave the voiding of power itself. We might say the Cave is a comedy, as Lacan says of *The Balcony*.[21] Aristotle, who categorized these things that Plato demonstrated to us as thought, argued that Comedy was born of the processions integral to the festivals of Dionysus, the leaders of which Aristotle calls *phallika* precisely because they carried large images of 'pricks' *en route* – to use the colloquialism Genet prefers when referring to the Chief of Police, the 'prick of great stature' at the head of the 'democratic' festival of the brothel.[22] But Plato is no nihilist. This void comedy exposes at the heart of naked power the impotence the prick stands (in) for, that must be thought through, given its subject and, thus, its proper form.

The Prisoners – that is, *us*, we good citizens, subject-support for the power of the 'prick of great stature' – do not, the Cave analogy contends, have the ready means of this thought. Although, as consequences will show, we do have the capacity to think it: as *The Balcony* indicates *vis-à-vis* the revolt, the truth of this thought rages along outside. Precisely, the knowledge of the city, the images on the Cave wall, and the means of its reproduction – the techniques of the masters of the things of stone and wood, preclude this thought or the orientation to this 'inexistent' thought, as the very condition of possibility of such a Cave/State, such a political configuration, which is, let's face it, 'our democracies'. It's not that this thought, which cannot be thought, goes un-represented in the democracy, which is, of course, the paradigm of representation for Plato (where constitutions proliferate in the market place): it is that it *is* represented that is the issue. In *The Balcony*, it is only the Police Chief who, as he says, 'penetrates through to this reality that the game offers' inside the Cave, while the rebels take aim from outside, and, *as such*, are unable to score.[23]

The promise of democracy, that it is for all or, more pointedly, the truth of this all, politically speaking, is precisely what is corrupted in representation such that the very thought-truth of democracy – justice, to speak philosophically, participation without image – remains the impossible kernel of democracy itself. Democracy, Plato is saying, insists precisely because the real of what it represents is conceived as impossible to attain. Representative democracy reproduces itself interminably in relation to this impossibility, and in turn it precludes justice, what is real of it, from ever being truly manifest. This truth of democracy *must* remain inexplicable for it. Thus the character of Plato's escapee, forced to be free, as it were, by his encounter with the inherent lack in the excess of images is a figure of the highest impiety, a singular character, unheard of and unseen, precisely because he refuses to give in before the regime of the 'inexplicable'.[24] As Badiou notes, 'the word "democracy" concerns what I shall call authoritarian opinion. It is forbidden, as it were, not to be a democrat.'[25] Democracy thus stages, night after night, as it were, in scene after scene, the impossibility of its possibility. An education in the impossibility of what founds it is the theatre of the state. Genet captures this fallacy in the following exchange:

Carmen He demands a true revolt. And dirty glasses.

Irma They all want everything to be as true as possible. . . .
Minus something indefinable, so that it won't be true.[26]

In terms of the 'analogy', the prisoners may compare to or correspond with or 'imagine' the citizen as audience and so too – under the sway of this knowledge of the orators, lawyers, politicians, businessmen, poet-educators – the 'middle class', as Badiou describes it in this text, those whose knowledge, 'constitutional' and 'resistant', gives the democratic city its norms, its images, and its limits. For Badiou, the middle classes 'participate naïvely in the formidable inegalitarian corruption of capitalism, without even having to know it. Others, a very small number, higher up, will know it for them.'[27] This is what the Police Chief knows. But it's not capitalism that is at issue, which is not a politics, but rather 'our democracies' and thus, as Badiou says in *Metapolitics* apropos of what philosophy must be: 'If "democracy" names a supposedly normal state of collective organization or political will, then the philosopher demands that we examine the norm of this normality. He will not allow the word to function within the framework of authoritarian opinion.'[28] But how can democracy function other than as it is known?

In *Rhapsody for the Theatre*, Badiou makes an illustrative distinction: a *viewer* is what the cinema constitutes, while the Theatre constitutes a *spectator*. Hence:

> Let's say that a spectator is real, whereas a viewing public is merely a reality, the lack of which is as full as a full house, since it is only a matter of counting. Cinema counts the viewers, whereas theatre counts on the spectator . . . So theatre is an affair of the State, which is morally suspicious, and requires a spectator. That much we know . . . The Spectator: Point of the real by which a spectacle comes into being and which, as Regnault tells us, corresponds to the taciturn and haphazard evening visitor. As pure 'count' the viewer cannot be subject; taciturn and haphazard the spectator is a figure of chance and as such may become 'subject'.[29]

As pure 'count', a viewer cannot be subject. Taciturn and haphazard, thus dialectically 'available', so to speak, the spectator is a figure of chance. Such chance is unpresentable and, as such, a possible 'subject'.[30] Subject to theatre, the spectator is the figure of a 'generic humanity', a 'humanity subtracted from its differences' and, again as such, inimitable. Can such a figure be thought? For Badiou, this is what the theatre thinks – that it be thought. For

Plato, whose gesture makes Badiou's thought possible, it is this un-thought of theatre that must be.

There can be no image of what a polity is not: even if the image is itself never what there is of itself. Re-presentation, as the word itself tells us, acts on that which must in some way already be present. It acts on it to make its existence *known*, or perhaps to make known *its* existence. The thought which animates Plato's cavernous little production – one among many instances of his rivalry with the poets, by saying in a few words what they don't or won't say in tens of thousands? – is that the thought of something otherwise than this knowledge of democracy, this limit of what can be thought as politics, nowhere exists. It is the void at the heart of all representation which representation, precisely as an image, shows us to be there. This is the crux of the matter. Hence the dialogue predicates itself on an *inexistence*, which, not even being presented, cannot be represented. There is no polity extant which escapes the power of representation or the re-presentation (imitation) of that which presents (model) to us what there is (Idea) as such. The *Republic*, the world of the cave turned upside down and inside out like an old sock, is the invention of this inexistence. It is nothing become everything, wherein representation is no longer the means of (the) production. The *Republic* is, incontrovertibly, the Theatre of the Idea.

The Cave, then, *analogizes* only the fullness of the polity in so far as it is the form of representative reproduction, a pedagogy of interests, representing the interests of 'democracy' as being in the interest of its audience. This reduction of knowledge to interest is one of Plato's key topics and targets. But it then also must analogize the void at the heart of the polity, what inexists for it and is included as such. The Cave is thus a study in what must *not be* for the State, what is not counted anywhere to exist, what is off limits to knowledge, and what must not come to be at all costs. This gives to the Cave what we can now call its *pornographic topology*.

Plato portrays Socrates, across the breadth of the dialogues, and across Athens, as the atopic and abnormal character of this nowhere existing city state who, incorporating into him this very inexistence ('I know nothing', 'I don't teach', etc.), must not be for the city – lest his character become the site of new and manifest production, lest the activity of the spectator become the subject of participation. The Cave 'corresponds', then, to nothing – to that which is nothing at all, and is thereby the site for the truly free citizen, one subject to justice as the truth of all. What sort of image has no referent, what is representation without that of which it is a re-presentation?

For Plato, this is what theatre lacks by its very form: access to what there is as such; thus, to any new subject and any new form of the city. By contrast, theatre can stage the image in all its nudity. In the play by Genet, this is the power of the Police Chief: 'the un-seductive emblem of the power [*puissance*] with which naked power [*pouvoir*] animates seductive images'. But the Police

Chief is not nothing – which is the problem. This prick is everywhere the real potency of the image.

So, to reiterate: the question of this nothing is staged in the Cave, the question of that which is without image. Plato presents, alongside the fullness of the city – the city as it represents itself to itself – an image of nothing, which is to say, no image at all. The Cave is a piece of theatre of the city: of the city as it is, in terms of the knowledge of it that exists as such – 'in every way believe that the truth is nothing other than the shadows'[31] – and, more critically, of that which for this same city is impossible to be and so, given its knowledge is that of representation, impossible to know. Theatre, which requires writing, never ceases unwriting itself, Badiou avers, yet, at the same time, 'no other art form is able to pin down the intensity of what *happens* the way Theatre does' (emphasis added).[32] Yet Theatre's capacity to fix the intensity of the event is bound up with the risk of dissimulation and misdirection.

So the formalization of this nothing that happens, this impossible-to-know staged in and by the Cave, is what is thought through as the Republic itself under the *mathematical* and not the theatrical condition: A mathematical method [is] subtractive of the reign of images precisely in the way it analyses the reign of images. It opens up the image to the thought it forecloses from being so. So 'analogy' might not be the word for the Cave, finally. Or it might fall short of saying what there is.

Perhaps, as we have been suggesting, it is a theatre of the Cave, if, that is, we can accept that it is possible that theatre be that which stages this gap between what is and what is not in the single and same act. The theatre of the city and the 'Theatre' of what it is to have done with this 'theatre' of the city: 'Theatre is the figurative reknotting of politics, and this regardless of its subject matter.'[33] It is a production of non-performance, a 'heresy' as Badiou notes, and as Socrates, our exemplary citizen-actor, stands charged. As such, it puts before us the necessity of decision – for Plato, the decision to *formalize* what inexists as the knowledge of representation (the Socratic heresy) – but, and this is Badiou's intervention into Platon*ism*, theatre does not itself decide. It stages the decision to be made – for what there is, or for what there is not (yet).

For Plato, in effect, the failure of the theatre of the city, or the lack it performs, and hence the reason he stages his own acts as unstaged dialogues, is its already decided form. To be the knowledge of representation makes the theatre nothing more than another form of sophistry, of oratory, of interest, of established norms, of the culture industry so beloved of the well-schooled bourgeoisie and so critical for their projected image. Which is to say, as Plato well knows, this theatre is not a passive form, but a reproductive one. Hence, paradoxically, this State theatre is not supposing an already-constituted subject, the subject who simply experiences theatre, attends its affects and then goes back home to his or her bourgeois comforts as usual. This is an Aristotelian inflection, an affect in itself, itself under the sway of the always-already-taken decision for the norm of the middle, the un-golden mean. For Plato, by contrast, theatre was a real force in the *creation* of the subject as such, the subject of representation, of established knowledge and, critically, of the guardian of the limits of established knowledge: *this* subject as all there is to know. Plato had no illusions as to the power of the theatre of the poets in remaking every day, in policing, the role of the democratic subject and hence our democracies. Paradoxically, *this* theatre will not contradict one's objective individuality.

Paradigmatically, Socrates, the alienable figure of the true, is killed by this State theatre. Which is also to say that the show trial was true: Socrates does indeed corrupt the youth. It's just that for Plato – who re-stages the show trial across the entirety of the dialogues – Socrates corrupts theatrical corruption itself. In *The Clouds*, Aristophanes had made Socrates the comical figure of the corruption of the city, making him effectively unpresentable. Like Genet's Police Chief, but in reverse, no one must come to play the role of the corruptor *par excellence*, the buffoon for whom knowledge is lacking. So the city kills him as the figure whose singular and abnormal corruption threatens the 'truth' of the city. Comedy does its work or has its effect, as Lacan argues, making the un-representable *appear* as impossible, ineffable, inexplicable. But the comedy of the theatre is not the truth of the philosopher, even if they aim, whether blindly or deliberately, at the same thing. The phallic function of naked power is not the void site of an event, but its all-too-apparent lack. The former is the condition of the present representation, its very unconditionality; the latter is the becoming true of a present without image, a city in discourse, but not impossible, demanding its subject.

Plato's objection is that the theatre of the poets, the theatre of the state, is the highest conceit in so far as it supposes it knows what cannot be known. This is what it stages, what it teaches as what is essentially sacred to it. It proselytizes the inaccessible, the inexplicable for us: not the *impossibility* at the heart of all knowledge, but the *knowledge* of impossibility itself. It teaches impotence in the face of what there is, which is to say, the positive incapacity of the subject. This knowledge is excessive and precisely in the way of imitation. It at once supposes what it is an image of and supposes that there is no access to it other than through the image, but at the same time the image is something more than that of which it is the image – this must be presupposed.

It is that thing in its appearance as that thing alone, and is more than it is by being its image. The image relies on that which it imitates to be that which is impossible otherwise to know. It is the guarantee that there is no other knowledge. It is no accident Plato returns the favour done to Socrates by giving Aristophanes, that 'music-hall producer', hiccoughs in the *Symposium*.[34] Plato makes a comedy of Aristophanes or with him, perhaps, making him the pause after the absurdity of Pausanias and putting the medical man in his place. 'Cure me or take my turn', Plato makes Aristophanes declaim.[35] A talking cure. As Lacan notes, 'it's a crudity, a gag, a sending in of the clowns'.[36] Plato dialecticizes Comedy itself – he makes comedy of the comedian's comedy. This demands a new form.

Thus Plato's love of mathematics which represents nothing, mere lines in the sand inscribing what this nothing is: diagonals, slaves, ignorance, impiety. Plato does not think the theatre as a site of knowledge in truth but subtracts thought from the theatre as that which shows, precisely, where such a knowledge in truth is not. The theatre marks out, as we said, where *there is* that which cannot be. In Comedy, the *phallika*, the prick of great stature, is always the sure sign of the impotence it hides. But this requires another thought to be thinkable for Plato, which is what mathematics is for him. Hence the old polemic: mathematics versus the poem.

In so far as the ideal city is concerned, the poets will cease to be what they are in so far as the truth of the ideal needs no representation and its spectator manifests as subject. For Plato, the ideal city is the site wherein the Idea presents itself in each and every action of the players – it's a short-circuiting of representation, which is left out of the account. These players – 'all the world's a stage', as Jaques ironizes in Shakespeare's *As You Like It* – these citizens model the Idea, they do not represent it (thus producing that which is in excess of it and thus is not it). As noted, the poets are not so much expelled from the Ideal City, they simply have no place there, or they have no knowledge of it – they wither away – and, as such, the Ideal City is the city in which the theatre as the site of this knowledge has become nothing. The just city, being for all, is more democratic in truth than any democracy, which, in its 'splendour' is always both one thing *and* its other.[37] Yet this city is subtractive of democracy.[38]

The prisoner (the spectator become subject), as is so often overlooked, does not simply escape from the city, aided and abetted by a ready-to-hand *deus ex machina*, even if it is that he (or she) is dragged out! But, as never happens, our prisoner comes back down into the Cave as rebel. Hence the commonly claimed contemporary analogy with cinematic reproductions such as Bruce Beresford's *The Truman Show*, for example, miss the point entirely, and in two key ways: truth is not the ascent of an individual, an individualism, a meritocracy. 'Thinking for one's self', as individualism would have it, is not the aim. It's also not a catharsis of the spectator, a revelation nor an affect. Rather, it's a collective (re)orientation to what is possible for us. Philosophy is itself an action, as Plato conceives and invents it – what can be thought as truly manifest is what can be for all.[39] Every dialogue plays this out.

Moreover, and this is what Genet also stages in *The Balcony*, Hollywood, the contemporary brothel of images, as Baudrillard effectively argues, exists in order to make the 'reality' that surrounds it appear by contrast as the Real itself, when in fact our contemporary reality is effectively this brothel of images as such, and as such it is the means of escape from the Real *while*, more tellingly, being also the cover of this escape.[40] As Carmen, Madame Irma's right-hand woman, as it were, replies to her bosses' question regarding her 'scruples' in spying on the girls and clients: 'Entering a brothel means rejecting the world. Here I am and here I stay. Your mirrors and orders and the passions are my reality.'[41] Hollywood is the image of this reality of mirrors and orders. This productive impossibility of the Real satisfies and suffices, in so far as we know only the freedom of desire, which, as Lacan, the arch-Platonist, notes, is the freedom finally to desire in vain. This slavish desire for what appears as appearance is the homiletic knowledge of *The Truman Show*, and is thus anathematic to both the philosophical theatre of the Cave and the Theatrical truth of *The Balcony*. Theatre and philosophy are irreducible to the theatre which represents them.

The Balcony explores this contest of the power of the image, the image as the whole of the real, as what returns interminably, in which, finally, in an act of what Badiou laments as the 'eternal return' of the tomb, Roger, the rebel figure of the Real of the revolt outside, bursts into the brothel and asks to play the role of Police Chief, the 'prick of great stature': to, in effect, as is his right of representation, take him to his limit. Roger thus castrates himself while everyone looks on. But this too is an image – smoke and mirrors – and thus the Chief of Police dismisses the castration of the image everywhere imagined, as the incapacity to 'handle the role'. 'So which of us is washed up? He or I?', he asks, grabbing his prick and balls![42] As he says: 'I'll make my image detach itself from me. I'll make it penetrate into your studios, force its way in, reflect and multiply itself.'[43]

Badiou eschews the pessimism of Genet's conclusion – a pessimism seemingly shared by Plato in the Cave story, if not in the Republic itself, hence the distinction theatre/philosophy – which is, we might say, too wedded to the repetition of the act as against the truth of it, which it stages. Yet Badiou also avows, for this very reason, that it is the theatre as Theatre alone that can stage this decisive contest for us. In this sense, Genet, à la Mallarmé,[44] has at least as much in common with the drama of Plato – the theatre of ideas and of events and of a public yet constituted – as that of the comedy of Aristophanes in which the eternal phallus exposes itself to what it lacks. 'A modern comedy', Badiou says, 'should tell us where we are in terms of what is socially serious and in terms of its dissolution.'[45] Castration, Lacan says, in the Seminar in which he discusses Genet's piece, is 'at the heart of the dialectic of man'.[46]

As Badiou notes in *Handbook of Inaesthetics*, for Plato it is not philosophy as such that is the rival to the poets, but mathematics. Plato rejects poetry for mathematics as the condition of philosophy, for thought that is – he refuses it be knowledge; that is all and this all is a lot. Presentation versus representation, we might say, using and abusing some Badiouan terminology, model versus copy. One 'stages' the Idea without loss; the other exceeds the idea as loss. But let's be clear. For Plato, as Badiou argues, 'poetry is not directly opposed to the intellect, to the intuition of ideas. It is not opposed to dialectics, considered the highest form of the intelligible [and indeed which is essential to Theatre][46] ... what Poetry forbids is discursive thought, *dianoia*'. Badiou continues:

> Plato says that 'he who lends an ear to it must be on his guard fearing for the polity in his soul.' *Dianoia* is the thought that traverses, the thought that links and deduces. The poem itself is affirmation and delectation – it does not traverse, it dwells on the threshold. The poem is not a rule bound crossing, but rather an offering, a lawless proposition.[47]

As a self-declared Platonist, then, what can be the terms of Badiou's own fidelity to the theatre, to his encounter with it, to it, as a poetical, evental, condition for philosophy? It is a fidelity that does not preclude a fidelity to mathematics (the measure, weight and number that Plato opposes to the poem)[48] and that, between the two, makes emerge a vision of politics similarly subtracted from the dominance of representation. In other words, how can a Platonist not *oppose* the law and *logos* to pleasure and pain, the intelligible to affect?

It would seem that in terms of the fidelity to theatre that Badiou maintains he has, as Platonist, set himself an irreconcilable problem. But in effect this is his Platonism as such. For Plato, impasse or aporia was not the end of all thought but the impetus to think again.[50] Hence, whereas Plato determines philosophy to be the overcoming of this *opposition* in so far as one is the end of the other (even if he himself deploys images at the limit of *dianoia* to do so),[51] Badiou proposes the undoing of the opposition itself as the possibility of thought thinking itself. Badiou stages the division in thought between discourses not as opposition but as aporia, and thus recommences to think what is at stake in it. He takes Plato's lesson to Plato himself. Like the slave boy with whom Socrates stages a demonstration of its effect in the *Meno*, Badiou *diagonalizes* the terms at stake.

In the seminar published in 1982 as *Theory of the Subject*, Plato was still named by Badiou as the idealist *par excellence*, a founder in fact. This is in line with the long lineage of reception taken up into Marxism.[52] As noted, in the manifesto which supports and polemicizes the radical overhaul of metaphysics hitherto, Badiou declares himself Platonist. But this manifest Platonism is a qualified, indeed radicalized, Platonism in so far as what has stood as Plato in terms of the philosophical reception – both pre- and post-Nietzsche's intervention as 'overcoming' – must itself be done with. Anti-Platonism, Badiou is saying, opposes itself to an image of Plato called Platonism. It misrecognizes what is as its image and prosecutes the case of the rise of the simulacrum and the end of the Idea in opposition to what it misrecognizes. It is an ironically befitting approach for a discourse which, in Badiou's estimation, is a contemporary sophistry – powerful, educational, brilliant and linguistic in essence. By contrast, then, Badiou's Plato is not a Platonist, and Badiou's Platonism is not a return to essence but what in Plato remains 'invariant' for any possible philosophy. It is twofold, and, he says, a 'Platonism of the multiple'. So it is not One. As 'gesture', it has the force of an orientation. It is, as such, 'a new word in Europe', and thus it has neither referent nor knowledge. Yet, in making it so, the gesture brings it to exist from out of what has not been said of it.

Let us summarize this position, marking the decision and the gesture, the declaration and the caution, and tracing quickly the terms of their conjuncture. For as we have effectively been arguing, it is Plato after all who allows Badiou to treat the theatre in truth as the site of the new present. For Badiou to be Platonist is to be faithful to both the mathematical *conditioning* of thought and to insist, against sophistic nostalgia for the unicity of the flux, that 'there are truths'. So that there be something other than opinion, the encyclopaedia of established knowledges, or the 'state'. Such truths are rigorously *subjective*. Badiou's Platonism affirms 'an ontology of the pure multiple without renouncing truth, the truth of the subject'.[53]

For philosophy to return to itself, as Badiou puts it, and thus not be reconciled to its end or to the interminable display demanded by sophistry, requires it take up and reconfigure the means of its division from both. Hence Badiou reaffirms the Platonic institution of the speculative and formal divisions between being and appearing, truth and opinion, philosophy and sophistry, mathematics and poetry; a formal demonstration of what constitutes philosophical discourse as a *practice* of separation, division *and* invention; as *subtractive* of all forms of 'knowledge', thereby holding in abeyance both 'the tutelary figure of the One'[54] and the resigned conservatism of the 'rhetoric of instants'.[55] These founding acts of philosophy, the dialogues addressed to all, constitute a new public and not an audience *per se*, situating themselves within the conditions of mathematics, art, love and politics, wherein the truths of which we are capable are played out. To 'return philosophy to itself' is to break with the sophistic (in) varia of the past century or so – presence, meaning, finitude, objectivism, relativism, vitalism, and those for whom the affirmation of multiplicity must be the ruin of the category of truth. To philosophize is to formalize anew, each and every time the conditions allow, the consequences of this break without occluding the contingent and constitutive necessity of such a break.

At the end of his major work, *Being and Event*, Badiou asserts that, given what he has set out in this work, it is now possible to interrogate the history of philosophy in order to expose such categories as 'the event and the indiscernible at work but unnamed throughout the metaphysical text'.[56] Plato's dialogues, the series of enquiries into the *real* possibility of a non-sophistic way of life, so long buried under centuries of received wisdom, practised indifference, linguistic manipulation or regarded as the site of a necessary overcoming, are then re-dialecticized by such an interrogation. The Platonic *corpus* resumes again as the place of subjective enquiry.[57] As noted above, what is proper to philosophy is 'to conceive of the present'.[58] We can delineate Badiou's 'Platonic gesture' in three terms: orientation, situation and trajectory. A fourth, participation, knots these three together and is the conceptual core of this return. Participation is what summons the spectator, constituted by theatre, to what is possible for it Ideally.

In an interview accompanying the English translation of *The Concept of Model*, Badiou identifies 'participation' – the 'Platonic concept par excellence'[59] – as that which is at stake in the formalization of a model.[60] Roughly, a model creates both the conceptual space and the formal processes whereby the participation of the sensible in the intelligible can be thoug ht. Platonism, as Badiou conceives it, is both the 'knowledge of ideality' and 'the knowledge that access to ideality is only through that which participates in ideality'.[61] Or: 'the Idea is the occurrence in beings of the thinkable'.[62] Plato, in maintaining the 'co-belonging' or 'ontological commensurability' of 'the knowing mind and the known', effects thereby the radicalization of Parmenides' injunction 'that it is the same to think as to be'.[63]

In *Logics of Worlds*, this is translated as: 'The universal part of a sensible object is its participation in the Idea.'[64] To pre-empt and return at once, participation is something like the mode of the non-relation between the assemblage of theatre as Art and a philosophy under conditions.

What is consistently at stake in this 'dialectic of formalization' – the generic construction of a present – is the question of universality, how what is is – *and*, given that the Idea is not One, must *be* for all.[65] Badiou shares with Plato the conviction of the equal otherness of all others before the Idea, which true subjective participation – the definitive contrary to nostalgic submission – reveals within the realm of the sensible which nominally occludes it. The ramifications of participation – the activation in thought of the Idea – are present in all efforts to think real universality, for which, unlike thinkers of totality or presence, there are no privileged subjects even as there is always *some* subject.[66] For Plato in the *Republic*, and clearly staged, as we have argued, in the Cave, anyone, subject to the contingency of an event, has the capacity for truth.[67] As Badiou says in *Logics of Worlds*, participation names the 'affirmative joy which is universally generated by following consequences through'.[68] This is an *affect* external to the passive or even pacifying affects on an audience of theatrical reproduction, which, as we noted, stages what must be decided in its lack. The move from viewer-subject to subject-spectator is the move from catharsis, which returns us to our ordinary self-satisfaction, to 'restricted action', which is to be actively struck by an Idea of which we have no knowledge.[69] Thus, and apropos of *The Balcony*:

> The obstacle in the path of a contemporary comedic energy is the consensual refusal of all typification. Consensual 'democracy' is horrified by every typology of the subjective categories that compose it. Just try to take a pope, a great media-friendly doctor, the bigwig of some humanitarian institution, or the head of a nurse's union, and make them squirm upon the stage, burying them in ridicule! We possess infinitely more taboos than the Greeks did. It is necessary, little by little, to break them.[70]

The *orientation* of Badiou to Plato is twofold: philosophical action does not aim at definition or interpretation but *transformation*. Philosophy is the *discourse* of the possibility of transformation: that truths are real, that truth, which is not knowledge, is possible. Philosophy composes out of the singularity of its conditions, the *form* of transformation, conceptualizing, and thereby preserving, the infinite or invariant truth of the various finite and particular procedures which 'change the world'. 'Philosophy does not produce truths', Badiou says, but is provoked into being by events outside itself whose truths the conditions enact.[71] Philosophy is the discourse which seizes and composes the being-*there* of these truths. For both, the 'things' of the world are provocations *to philosophy*. For Plato, the (life-long) trial and eventual death of Socrates provokes the singularity of his turn to philosophy – away, ironically, from theatre – and manifest in the question 'how are we to live?' Badiou, similarly provoked by conservative renegations of all types, reinvigorates this same polemic at the heart of philosophy when he declares that he has 'only one question: what is the new in a situation?'[72] These questions convene a practice, the act of thought, and not a space of reflection.

This thinking of the *generic* (the new, the ideal or true) is the thinking through of 'the established situation' as oriented by the universal prescription inherent to *what happens* – what happens by chance happens *for* no one, for no-one-knowledge, and so happens for anyone at all. In order to effect the trace of the new in any *situation*, the situation itself *qua* 'structured presentation' must be (re)thought or 'worked through'. In the *Cratylus*, Plato – beginning with things and not words – provides the dialectical formula: 'I think we have to turn back frequently to what we've already said, in order to test it by looking at it backwards and forwards simultaneously.'[73] Thus *back* to the situation – its logical construction and its ontological predication – and forward from the Idea whose truth manifests itself in accord with, yet as aleatory exception to, that which is elemental to its situation.

In Plato's dialogues, Socrates, the 'exemplary figure of thought', the aleatory and indeed abnormal character of the theatre of Ideas, who consorts with women and slaves, confronts various figures of 'knowledge', those Lacan calls, referring to *The Balcony*, the symbolic representatives of the 'human professions': orators, dramatists, professional men, demagogues, generals, and so on. Plato collects this seemingly diverse array of interlocutors, under the term 'patrons of the flux'.[74] Armed only with ignorance, thus with what they profess to lack, Socrates constantly provokes them to speak in their own name precisely because it is clear to him (and once the appearance of things is stripped away, it will be revealed as such) that his interlocutors speak for some doctrine or other. Invariably – when they are not the figures themselves – they represent the doctrine of the poets: Homer, Hesiod, Pindar, Simonides, or Heraclitus and his followers, or Protagoras and Gorgias. Parmenides alone escapes this gathering, but his commitment to the One is equally problematic for Plato.[75]

Badiou notes that Plato rejects the Parmenidean ontology of the indivisibility of the One in favour of a division in being that admits that 'the nothing is'.[76] Thus, as is demonstrated in the *Sophist*, what is not has being – which, as we saw, is what the Cave stages for us but does not analogize. For Badiou, this turns on the distinction made in the *Parmenides* between two types of multiplicity: *plethos* and *polla*. The first is inconsistent multiplicity, the second 'consistent' or 'structured' multiplicity. Plato deductively 'intuits' the former, Badiou notes, but lacks the means to its formalization. Instead, Plato has recourse to the 'astonishing metaphor of a speculative dream'.[77] The wager at the heart of Badiou's Platonism – at the limits of Plato's own desire to escape the theatre of limits – is that it is Cantor who will turn the dream into a paradise. In general, for the patrons of the flux (or becoming), in their various ways, to claim the truth of a distinction was an error against the right of perception. For these *Protagoreans*, there is known only 'better' and 'worse',[78] their relation is constitutive, and no 'fixed point' not 'measured by man' anchoring a situation to its being can legitimately be conceived.

In *Manifesto for Philosophy*, Badiou determines six categories of anti-Platonism, which for him essentially establish the knowledge of philosophy in the twentieth century.[79] What unites them is an accusation against Plato with regard to the real of what is philosophy: *change* for the vitalists, *language* for the analytics, *concrete social relations* for the Marxists, *negation* for the existentialists, *thought*, in as much as it is other than understanding for Heidegger, *democracy* for the political philosophers. What they have in common is: a commitment to language, its capacities, rules and diversity, such that language is the 'great transcendental of our times'.[80] This entails a commitment to the end of metaphysics and thus philosophy since Plato. Plato is the point of an inception that must be reversed. Or in other words, contemporary 'philosophy' as an anti-Platonism, effectively 'puts the category of truth on trial'.[81] In this respect, tragedy becomes farce.

However, Badiou agrees with two claims that arise from the contemporary critiques: Being is essentially multiple;[82] and that Plato does mark a singular and decisive point in the history of thought. With regard to the first point of agreement, to say being is multiple today is to say it falls under the regime of mathematics *qua* ontology and not 'language'. In regard to the second point, Plato is to be understood today as an *incitement to thought*, through whom thought is given 'the means to refer to itself as philosophical' and thus 'independently of any total contemplation of the universe or any intuition of the virtual'.[83] Plato is decidedly not the moment at which thought turns to despair or to the eternal return or to the rebel become cop; rather, it is Plato's conception of what *there is* out of what appears, that matters and what *there is* are truths, 'a regime of the thinkable that is inaccessible to th[e] total jurisdiction of language'. A 'Platonic gesture', conditioned by a 'Platonism of the multiple'.

The notion that truth is 'on trial' in contemporary philosophy is, as noted, entirely prescient. Plato, personally affected by the event of the trial – or rather 'the life of Socrates' it brought into relief – takes this as his central point of articulation, deciding thereby that an encounter between two incommensurable 'ways of life' has 'taken place', thus undermining the sophistic (and later, Aristotelian) inflection of difference as a global trait. In dialogue after dialogue – and by working through the various articulations of the 'encyclopaedia' – Plato elaborates the *indiscernible* consequences of Socrates' *non-sophistic* discourse. As we argued above, the universal form of this non-sophistic theatre is given ultimately in the *Republic*, the ideal city, the place where sophistry is 'assigned to its place', that is, where it withers away.[84] The trajectory is that of the step-by-step articulation of this 'immanent universalism' marked by 'Socrates', which crosses *and* subtracts itself from the contemporary sophistic city. Plato's dialogues each engage the 'encyclopaedia', taking their cue from the sophists and anti-philosophers in order to begin to think *through* what it is they propose in order to make it possible that this thought be thought otherwise: specifically, with regard to its *Form*.

Likewise, Badiou notes that to return philosophy to itself *today*, one must take: from Heidegger, the importance of the ontological question; from the analytic philosophers, the 'mathematico-logical revolution of Frege-Cantor'; from deconstructive-postmodernism, the inexistence of the one of totality; and, from Marx and Lacan's anti-philosophies, a modern doctrine of the subject (BE 2). Badiou seeks to free what is essential in these discourses from the predicates which constrain them, in order to compose a new philosophical form *for our present age* that is simultaneously concerned with what philosophy 'had for a long time decided to be, a search for truth'.[85]

For Plato *and* Badiou, philosophy, to be anything other than a branch of sophistry – for Plato, the inheritors of the poetic tradition – needs recourse to a discourse which cannot be reduced to the vicissitudes of opinion, dissemination without limit, the temper of the times, judgement, the play of languages, or, in short, the state of the situation. This is why mathematics must again be 'foundational' for philosophy. It is *the* singular discourse which, 'in one and the same gesture, breaks with the sensible and posits the intelligible'. It thus denies, *by* its formal existence, the right of *doxa* to elevate its knowledge into the 'truth of [an] era'.[86]

In what we might call the 'contingency of recommencement', each time Plato opens a dialogue it is in some way already faithful to this mathematical idea that discerns the split between the *noetic* and the *somatic*, between thought as a disciplined procedure of participation in the Idea and *doxa* as the ingenious reconstruction of the continuity of the state as a stable and fixed body of knowledge. Plato's recourse to mathematics – as aporetic as it *had* to be – is not so much a 'mathematical turn', but the realization that only mathematics can consistently support thinking what is otherwise *indiscernible* to a situation. Plato deploys the force of its demonstrations to extend the intuitions and implications opened up by the Socratic *encounter* with the sophistic State. The risk of philosophy amounts to accepting that a discourse exists that does rationally and consistently *think* the being of situations, thus providing the anterior, apodictic and formal Idea of the truths that 'found' them.[87] Philosophy thinks the truths that exist. It is the site for their composition as discourse.

Similarly, and with regard to this sort of encounter, in his *Theses on Theatre*, refusing that theatre settle for the blandishments of commercialization into a salaried profession, like all the others, and refusing also to be subject to the dictates of well-placed and servile functionaries of the state, Badiou, following this Platonic logic of subtraction from established doctrine and its reproduction, argues that:

> The duty of the theatre is to recompose upon the stage a few living situations, articulated on the basis of some essential types. To offer our own time the equivalent of the slaves and domestics of ancient comedy – excluded and invisible people who, all of a sudden, by the effect of the theatre-idea, embody upon the stage intelligence and force, desire and mastery.[88]

To 'return philosophy to itself' is then to combine in a singular discourse the thinking of the act of interruption which theatre, for example, stages as Idea, *and* the formalization of its consequences. For Badiou, given 'our situation' – a state that knows by way of images and repetition – it is necessary to do what Plato did. But to do what Plato did is to do it pursuant to the contemporary conditions of the present age. For Badiou, the injunction to attend to the 'contemporary conditions' requires a different conceptual attitude to mathematics and poetry. We know what Plato thinks about poetry (and its sophistic variants), how its charms are precisely what must be guarded against – for the *coincident* good of the individual soul *and* the polity – and for Plato, it is this very affect which means that poetry cannot ultimately be considered as a thought (*dianoia*) of its own. For Badiou, by contrast, poetry thinks and the theatre thinks, and philosophy, as the thinking of these thoughts, does not annul poetry and theatre *as* thought.[89] For Badiou, poetry can both think the sense of its own situation and, within the space of philosophy, command a position equal to mathematics in so far as poetry, even theatre, names the event as Idea – the very sign of the mathematical impasse – and opens a fictional space within which the situated indiscernible or generic (love of) truth will come to 'be-there'. We are back, almost, to Plato's theatre of the Cave.

While Plato endorses the interruptive capacity of mathematics, his problem is that mathematics cannot be anything other than this. This is to say, mathematics has no *choice* but to break with opinion. For Plato, this signifies a lack of freedom in mathematics; there thus remains a certain obscurity in regard to its understanding of what it thinks, and this prevents it from being properly '*noetic*'. How can the truth of the break which mathematics establishes with opinion be thought in such a way that the obscurity it bequeaths to philosophy be illuminated in terms of a principle which serves thought at its most extensive? Plato cannot answer this question and so, Badiou says, for him dialectics names a second break: the break with the 'obscurity of the first' break.[90]

This *breaking* with the obscurity of the first break is no longer required today, Badiou contends, because mathematics thinks *its* situation (as presentation of presentation); it is autonomous and in no way in need of philosophy's imprimatur. Gödel's theorem demonstrates that mathematics, as with all situations, is structured *and* incomplete – thus an inconsistent multiplicity, precisely in so far as it forms a consistent discourse. As set theory demonstrates, the former – 'the nothing that is', let's say – is essentially the very condition of the latter and, as such, this 'obscurity' does not annul or condemn mathematics to non-knowledge, but instead comes to define its internal rigour and consistency. Philosophy situates this thought as the very site of its own capacity to think the universal trajectory of what is generic to situations – a truth being precisely that which is generic and therefore must *address* every element of the situation for which it is a truth. Thus the impasse or aporia of ontology – that being is not One – is crucial to philosophy's *multiple* composition. Philosophy in this sense is, like its theatrical condition, an assemblage. Moreover, the very idea of an assemblage, its consistency as such, has an ontological veracity. So we know what an assemblage is, its event can be demonstrated:

[T]heater is an assemblage. It is the assemblage of extremely disparate components, both material and ideal, whose only existence lies in the performance, in the act of theatrical representation. These components (a text, a place, some bodies, voices, costumes, lights, a public ...) are gathered together in an event, the performance [representation], whose repetition, night after night, does not in any sense hinder the fact that, each and every time, the performance is evental, that is, singular. We will therefore maintain that this event – when it really is theatre, the art of the theatre – is an event of thought. This means that the assemblage of components directly produces ideas. These ideas – and this point is crucial – are theatre-ideas.[91]

With regard to philosophy, theatre is in this case 'rescued' from sophistry, its discursive double, precisely by the constraining rigour of a mathematical ontology which, being incomplete to itself, induces the decided specificity of poetry's place. At the risk of sentimentality, Badiou returns philosophy to the conditions of Plato's speculative dream and thus to the question of that which is 'for all' but is not *one*: 'When all is said and done, theatre thinks, in the space opened between life and death, the knot that binds together desire and politics. It thinks this knot in the form of an event, that is, in the form of the intrigue or the catastrophe.'[92] For Badiou, taking up what Plato knew as what theatre demands, but whose means of truth he lacked, the denuding of the dream into the intelligible via the Idea is now not impossible.

This, as we have argued, is the orientation that Badiou takes to his study of *The Balcony*, in so far as *The Balcony* exposes in all its voluptuousness and phallic excess, the lack at the heart of the present. The democratic fetish, displayed everywhere in the slew of images that passes today as its discourse, is the repository of what is truly nothing for it. Thus, as Badiou avers, contrary to the contemporary fetish for a democratic theatre on stage and in parliament, of 'horror, suffering, destiny or dereliction':

> our question instead is that of affirmative courage, of local energy. To seize a point and hold it. Consequently, our question is less concerned with the conditions for a modern tragedy than with those of a modern comedy ... Our time requires an invention that would join. upon the stage. the violence of desire to the roles of small local powers. An invention that would communicate, through theatre ideas, everything of which a people's science is *capable*. We want a theatre of capacity, not of incapacity.[93]

And thus, as Vitez notes, 'the aim of theatre is to clarify our situation, to orientate us in history and life'.[94] This is to say, to make this nothing *be* from out of the contemporary brothel of *doxa* is the act of thought *par excellence*, and this act of subjective capacity is what the philosopher watches for in the affirmative productions of the theatre and in the excessive recesses of the state; with patience and delight, he or she weaves out of one the truth of the other, such that it will never not be impossible for us.

These, then, are the stakes of this brief pamphlet: to diagnose the pornography of the present age by philosophically interrogating a theatrical staging of the logics of its domination as democracy; and, through this diagnosis, to offer another way of deimagining the images that beset us, as a propaedeutic to justice.

Brothel as category

William Watkin

Something is missing

Stop. Rewind. Re-check the dates. Look again over your notes. There is surely something awry here somewhere, something important that is missing. Ask yourself: what is the order of representation, order in the sense of one thing that comes after another? Badiou's essay begins by speaking of philosophy and nostalgia, of the manner by which the present tense is often felt to be lacking, and how this means by definition the temporal category called contemporaneity is blighted by a sense of lack. Read these not so much as opening gambits than as clues, evidence that the piece itself is caught in a kind of temporal problematic in relation to Badiou's wider body of work. After all, this paper was delivered in 2013, an entire lustrum after *Logiques des Mondes* was published, so one would expect it to be dominated by the new vocabulary of that book, its logics of appearing. One might also expect the essay to concern itself with worlds in relation to being, attempting to articulate the most challenging part of Badiou's entire body of work to date, the ontological, or how sets and categories (worlds) can in some sense be articulated. In that *Logiques des Mondes* is a long book about the order of representation, then an essay primarily concerned with the order of representation will surely be a brilliant and surprising reading of the traditional allegories of the event Badiou made great use of before he discovered categories. Finally, most importantly, because this is an essay about the evental intimations of Genet's *The Balcony*, I would imagine now would be the most opportune moment to inform the Philosophy Forum of *France Culture* of Badiou's new conception of the event, as a self-belonging, self-mentioning category which impacts on the objective phenomenology of the actual infinities of our relational worlds.

Yet although by rights the piece should be dominated by the formalism that permeates *Logiques*, that mode of mathematics called category theory, in truth the essay itself does not use the term 'category' even once. Echoing Badiou's reading of Bluebeard in the final act of Messaien's opera,[1] or indeed Trump's famous stalking of Clinton in their televised campaign debates, it is as if *Logiques* is on stage, yet non-relatable. The overall effect of this, for me at least, is unsettling and undermining. I have staked my reputation on the centrality of *Logics of Worlds* to the understanding of the most important of all Badiou's ideas, that of the event. And while I am often struck how philosophers fail to live up to our vision of them, so that I have in the past made Foucault more Foucauldian, Agamben more Agambenian, accepting that there is many a slip twixt cup and lip, here we are not so much speaking of a slip of the tongue, as Badiou speaking in entirely the wrong language. A language of events that is ontological, rather than, as he himself makes clear, the true language of any comprehension of and adherence to events, the language of categories. Am I expected to correct or adjust Badiou, to make him true to his own body and trajectory of thought?

By my reading the message of the piece is that *The Balcony* defines a dialectic between the 'real' of revolutionary unrest outside the brothel and the order of representation within the brothel. This being the case, the brothel is a category and Genet's play ought to be unique in the means by which it expresses categorical relations, and the manner by which it treats the event as an impossible diagram within the purview of that category. The reading of *The Balcony* would most likely resemble those of *Bluebeard* and Roberts' painting in *Logiques*,[2] only with the evental category added in, not dissimilar in a way to his remarkable reading of seriality at the beginning of *Logiques* but this time tied to one work of art,[3] one perspective. Spurred on by these thoughts, I go back to the essay with a more receptive eye. I surveil the piece electronically in keeping with the times, doing searches for data-sets around my hashtags of categories, diagrams, envelopes, reverses, atoms, conjunction, degrees of intensity, transcendental functors, consequences and so on. None are trending. I am forced to confront the facts which show that rather than speak of the age, our age, in terms of categories, instead Badiou decides to speak of democracy in terms of pornography. How can this be? What relation is there between the two, especially when, in his definition of our age in *Logics*, pornography is never mentioned? I realize at this juncture that it is not textual exegesis that I committed to, but textual policing. A crime has been committed, a crime of omission, and armed as I am with a forensic knowledge of category theory as a means of formalizing and disrupting our conception of worldly situations, then it is apt, I suppose, that I have been put in charge of the investigation.

The questions is, how can you in all seriousness define our democratic age as being dominated by the term 'pornography'? The answer is, by categories alone. Which means we have a second line of enquiry to follow: why, given the publication date and subject matter, is this essay seemingly untouched by the formal means of *Logics of Worlds*? There is, in other words, a problem with the evidence we have, pornography and the age, and with that which has not presented itself at the scene of the crime, category theory. I put it to you, the jury, that there is only one way that our age could come to be implicated in the offensive crime of pornography, and that is by the application of category theory. And so I call the first witness: relation itself.

Relation

To think of one thing in terms of another has ever been the task of the philosopher, which is why Badiou's choice of category theory as the logical/mathematical base for his logics of appearing, his objective phenomenology, and his precondition for the manifestation of that rare beast, the event, is both prescient and historically grounded. For a category is nothing other than the mathematics of meta-structural relation between objects in the same world that, however, solves the logical paradoxes, impasses and aporias attendant on philosophies of the immanence of beings in a world since the Greeks. The real philosophical question, we glean from categories, is not to think of one thing in terms of another as regards properties they share in common in relation to a being that they do not, but rather to think of one thing in terms of how it acts on another, and how this functional relation defines worlds such as they are and differentiates beings not in terms of *what* they are, but what they do to each other.

A category is a transcendental function located in the least largest position above all of its components, these are called diagrams. It oversees the degrees of relationality between the objects in its line of sight, gifted to it by its position of only-just superiority, and is defined solely by being the transcendental least largest position from which all diagrams of a world can be related to by at least two objects: the object in relation to itself and the category the object is included in. Being visible is a function, the archetypal function. It means being held in a functional relation with at least one other object, such that this larger object acts on you with a basic existential operation: as a being, you exist, to some degree of intensity, in this world, relationally speaking. A category structures relations, between the diagrams it oversees, and between itself and all its diagrams, even if, within the world, these varied diagrams do not all relate to each other. The technical name for this vantage point of existential clumps is a partially ordered set, or POSet.

Which is why thinking about worlds rather than being is, by definition, political. To inspect, to monitor, to surveil, is always to create a functional relation of force from which a quanta of power emerges. In addition, the mode of regard enacts a functional change on its object. To treat one thing from the perspective of another, to think of the relation between things, not simply because they are differentially similar, but rather in terms of the spheres of influence between objects, subjects, statements, states, how one acts on another, how these two act on a third and how all three are corralled by a distant, perhaps infinite fourth, has surely always been the basis of a lasting idea of *Realpolitik*. Categories structurally compose power, not sovereign or revolutionary power, but something more akin to regulatory, managerial, indeed anonymously technocratic, low-level coercion. Such that if philosophy concerns relationality, if bringing things together is what it primarily does – isn't that what it means to extend a concept over an object or to speak of two things as part of the same set? – and if, in doing so, it always takes the higher ground, because that is where categories appear, then it is all but impossible not to think of a philosophy of worlds as *de facto* a politics. A politics of thought, presentation, communication and sanction of ideas in action within an enclosed world or state. Philosophy of this sort is a *nomos* forever extending its influence into the zone of anomie, step by step, object by object, functional relation by relation.

It is because any world is a POSet, that, unlike in sets, there is always room for more because a category is not larger than the world, it is always functionally defined as simply the next largest, which is what is meant by Badiou's term the 'transcendental functor'. Categories are not imperial, rather a category defines a territory by no other functional means than its being able to compose one by taking up the next highest position, and using that as a Panopticon that, in observing the relations between the things below, also combines them into a structurally stable world of functions, defined by the simple managerial value of slightly greater than, slightly more powerful, slightly more functional, slightly closer to the top than ... On this reading, the power structure of biopolitical states is categorical. Neoliberalism is categorical. The European Union is categorical. Evidence-based governance is categorical. The internet is categorical. Big tech is categorical. Whereas Trump and Brexit and populism and war are not. Nor, for that matter, are events.

What a thing actually is, and how it acts on another thing, without changing its 'essence' or that of the thing it is influencing, dominating, while being able to register that the existence of these two so-called things, is entirely dependent on what a thing does, not what it is, is the quintessence of the entirety of the Being and Event project up to the present moment.[4] And yes, there is a politics to this, one clearly expressed in the frantic closing pages of *The Pornographic Age*, a politics of the event, of subjects, truths, ethics and militancy, but there is also a politics of relation, nothing but a politics of relation, in that the two politics on view in the text concern relationality and non-relationality, or worlds taken as categories, and truths taken as non-relational diagrams of said categories. How things relate, the force of that, and how the non-relational makes its way within that world of forces, is the real basis of Badiou's politics and the topic of our text.

The Pornography → Democratic Age morphism

There is an intensity to the article that makes it hard to gain perspective and see the bigger picture. The piece is short, compressed, at times almost unbearable in its contractions. The entire significance of an idea often hangs on a word, or the contestation of a seemingly innocuous phrase. Yet, at the same time, the range is epic, its tasks Herculean. It defines our age, in terms of the concept of democracy, through the allegorical reading of a play, which describes an aesthetic category in terms of its economic corruption (pornography), which is mapped onto Lacanian theory, to fulfil an overall ontological consideration of the situation of being in-between events in terms of the non-relation between the world *qua* brothel and the real out there. It attempts, in other words, to stage the relation between a complex of concepts which, through the use of Genet's play, gives said concepts a visibility (relations can be seen, they appear on the stage) and an action (as ideas are performed by the actors on the stage), by placing them in an overarching and meaningful space (the brothel as setting). As the title of the play, *The Balcony*, suggests, Genet's play and Badiou's reading of it are all about finding a single vantage point from which to observe all these other elements literally in action.

This brothelized collection is disjunctively non-relational. The parts that compose the brothel-world are not parts that in any way traditionally go together. The air inside the brothel is stale, stultifying, objects crowd around, insisting on establishing unnatural relations with me, and with each other. They force themselves on me. I need a vantage point, higher ground, fresher air. I decide to take a turn on the balcony I saw on my way in here, I think this is the door . . . [opens a door, and goes on to the balcony].

Yes, from up here things are clearer. I realize, for example, that surely the basic point of Badiou's focus on the brothel is that our democratic age can be defined as pornographic, because it is the age of the image corrupted by money. Hence the title: *The Pornographic Age*. Pornography has a function on our age that will, in the first instance, change our relation to our own epochal self-conception. Yet immediately the relational mapping of these diverse constructs, temporality, politics, art, phallic power, the image, capital, and the event, makes one cautious. How can it be that our age can be defined as pornographic, because of a play, which self-consciously uses psychoanalytic theory, is also somehow a comment on the image because the phallus is described as 'appearing' by the playwright as a function of comedy, and because of the role of the imago and imaginary in Lacan, allowing us to define democracy as pornographic because ours is also an age of images and of money? It is as if *The*

Pornographic Age has taken up a purposefully non-relational function along the lines of, let's throw all these diagrams together and see if I can find a way to make them fit.

This is not a good way to construct an argument, but then it isn't an argument. Categories are something different to argumentation, first-order propositional logic, or even set theoretical ontology, because categories do not prove things through linear accrual of localized, analytical truths or retroactive axiomatic proofs, they simply show what the structures of relation are. In that everything is allowable in any world, because anything appearing in said world is relatable, if only to itself and the overall category as such, then the choice of diagrams or concepts you want to relate is literally indifferent: they could be anything. It doesn't matter what you choose to put on stage, because once on stage, the being of the multiples does not alter, but by being-there, treading the boards, their existence is entirely defined by the staged relations of this multiple in this world within the sphere of influence of all these other multiples that have appeared there in it. You can put anything you want on stage, but once cued up in front of the lights, said multiple cannot be anything you want, because it must always relate, and relationality is the very definition of what it means to be an object of existence, or what we used to call existent beings.

If choice is indifferently meaningless in worlds, all the same the provocation in the brothel-world is clear. Our most revered political institution reduced to a sordid brothelization. If, it suggests, you can put the brothel in the capitalized state, such that the brothel relates to said state, for example thanks to the appearance of the chief of police or the economic laws which the brothel shares with capitalism, and its abuse of the explicit image for financial gain, then this also, in some senses, places our democratic age in the brothel. This is why it is important that the essay is called *The Pornographic Age*. In category theory, this would be written the pornography of age, or the *P* of *A*, but by this would be meant the means by which the age is acted upon by the functions that bind it to pornography. In other words, in this diagram, pornography takes the higher position, that of influence over the age. Take pornography to be *P* and the age to be *A*; their relation would be *shown* like this, $A \rightarrow P$, but *written* like this, *P* of *A*. Which is why you need to see that relation; which is why the linearity of logical language is not to be entirely trusted; which is why relations must be staged, not just defined.

Why does visualization of the order matter? For two basic rules that determine all categorical relations, those of compossibility and association. Compossibility captures the composite nature of all relations. Even a basic relation between two otherwise isolated units in a world is a composite relation because of the presence of the third unit, the category itself, which has to be able to see all relations in its world. An isolated string, $A \rightarrow P$, is always appearing within a C, a world, a category. Nothing can appear in a world and not relate, nothing that is apart from events. The arrows of compossible relations determine the directions of functional force, and these arrows must travel in the directions determined by said world. It is $A \rightarrow P$, even when A also relates to a C, which may also relate to P, indeed will have to if C is the category. That said, the means by which you consider these composite relations, of which there are usually many as categories are in general defined by their large size, larger than infinity in fact,[5] is free, as long as it is associative.

To be associative means it doesn't matter which side of a function you consider first, as long as the linear order of the equation, and the parts within, is maintained. Sometimes you want to think about democracy first, even if functionally it comes after pornography. Sometimes you want to think about democracy in relation to the image. Even if the image also relates to pornography, you can. But at no point does this preference of regard change the overall structures of relation. 'The Age of Pornography' then is not so much a title as a diagram, it explains a structural precedence of asymmetry, pornography acts on democracy; a compossibility, if I want to I can embed the pornography $\rightarrow$ democracy morphism into larger or more distanced diagrammatic relations; and is associative, it doesn't matter how complex the diagram of relations becomes, this basic local morphism will not alter.

If the problem is not that of relation *per se*, anything can relate to anything else if they co-appear in the same world, should we not be asking of the philosopher something along the lines of: is the reading justified, not the reading so much as the mapping or overlay of these objects? Yes they can co-appear on stage, but is it meaningful to stage their encounters? To answer this, we need to consider the primary function of categorical relation in Badiou, namely degrees of intensity of relation. In that Badiou's main concern categorically is existence, specifically the articulation of being as multiple within a multiple, into beings as function on other beings, his main functional concern is to what degree does this multiple appear in this world through the intensity of its relation to other multiples that co-appear therein.[6] In a brothel, for example, the handles of a door undoubtedly appear, but to what degree of intensity in relation to our basic morphism? They may share nothing more in common with our age than the simple fact that they appear on the same stage because a brothel has to have doors. So it is that some of the elements of the brothel co-appear with other elements of democracy in such a way as pornography can be seen to have a functional effect on our age in a negative register. While others tell us nothing of our age. This is a function of cleansed data selection, and there is no one guiltier of choosing the artistic object to fit the theory than Badiou. Thus Badiou can stage the relation between our age and pornography if he so desires, but to what degree of intensity?

If, for example, he argues that they relate to each other with maximum intensity in this world, then this would show that the two most relatable objects in the world are pornography and our democratic age. But to achieve that, the degree of intensity that each object has towards itself may have to be diminished to an almost unrecognizable level. In category theory a thing appears in a world due to relational identity, as I said. A thing is the thing it is because of a functional operation it shares with another thing which also appears. Yet, at the same time, every object in a world appears only in relation to itself, and the category as a whole. These are the two related definitions of identity. A multiple appears through the relation of itself to itself functionally to differing degrees in different worlds. In a play concerned with incarceration, options, access, and the like, handles would self-identify to a powerful degree. Of all the functional relations the multiple-handle can have in a world, in such a play most of these will be realized. Such an intense appearance will also give the handle more opportunities to relate to a greater diversity of objects because handles are located much closer to the category of the play, meaning they are higher up with a greater perspective.

Our question then is, in order for our age of democracy and pornography to appear on the same stage, what does one have to do to the degree of their own self-identity to make this happen? Do they have to travel so far from a received sense of what these words mean that they become close to empty signifiers in the process? The wider argument – categories are always the wider argument, it would seem – is that a play can be used as a domain, onto which are mapped non-aesthetic conditions whose relations can be staged, their functions literally performed, but not necessarily in a manner that is functionally or structurally significant and meaningful. One justification for the appropriation of Genet is that the comedic nature of the play is a good means by which to make power appear, in the form of the Chief of Police, placing power within the brothel, emphasizing the 'pornographic' nature of democracy, and laying the workings of power bare, by literally denuding the chief, presenting him as a 'right cock', as we say in my home town, so that the force of the phallus appears on stage. Dramatic comedy, then, is one of the functional powers of staged relations in this instance. The play therefore has the potential to add something to the conversation on our current age, except that it was penned in the 1950s and the democracy of the monetized image, if it exists, is surely a product of later developments in globalization, neoliberalism and technology. In other words, as a presentation of *our* age, the diagram of 'image' and its exploitation that functionally composes pornography in Genet's work lacks self- and relational intensity when mapped onto our *current* age.

Then there is that word 'pornographic'. Is Badiou's definition of pornography accurate? Which in category theory means asking to what degree of self-intensity does it partake when it appears in this world in relation to that other appearing thing? His diagrammatic construction combines the brothel, the phallus, denuding the phallus, the role of the image in Lacan, and the economic exchange of the brothel, to create a sense that democratic power is a sordid exchange of money over sexualized imagery. This can be presented as a strong diagram, but is not a particularly solid definition of pornography in our world, it has to be said. Is it even the case that a brothel is pornographic, or that the denuding of the Chief of Police is a pornographic act? Pornography is not just the monetization of imagery, there has to be something about explicitness in there, I think, a consideration of power that is primarily gendered, and a relation between the image and physical/affective excitation. A pornography of something, then, is an explicit presentation of the function of imagery centring around an act that is designed to exploit the parties involved, to produce an emotional/physical response from the viewer that is somehow seen as compromised: a pornography of sex, a pornography of violence, ruin porn, pity porn, etc. This is how pornography usually appears functionally in our world.

If we reconsider the purpose of the piece, we have a problematic diagram of mappings: an epoch, a play, Lacanian thought, an aesthetic category, a theory of the image, a politics, and an ontology of the event. While the mapping itself is not a problem, all functional relations are possible and thus at root indifferentiated, the self-identity of the terms clearly is. It is not clear that our age or pornography appear in this diagram with anything like a significant degree of self-intensity. Then we have the wider task, which is can these different domains be mapped on to each other so that overall a potential truth, one to come, begins to appear in the very world where such a truth, that of politics for the people, has become corrupted? Can the outside of the brothel start to emerge inside the brothel in such a way as the political desire of the people outside is not bought and sold within the brothel of contemporary democratic practice? Badiou seems confident of this, performing a perfectly adequate four-part schema of the play as yet another allegory of the intermittency of the event that is totally in keeping with his basic ontology of the event in place since *Being and Event* (PA 49). But if there is an answer to this question, then it resides not within the terminology and techniques of his 1988 masterpiece, which seem at first glance to dominate the essay, but thanks to the language and structures of *Logics of Worlds*, a text which appears on the surface at least to be totally absent from the essay, as if all reference to the work had been systematically redacted under the auspices of some greater power. It is this crime of omission, you may recall, that led to my being caught up in this whole sordid business in the first place, an omission that Badiou equates with the categorization of our current temporality under the heading of the contemporary as temporal lack. Meaning, if we are unsure that our age is pornographic, are we not equally uncertain that our epoch is, well, our epoch, our contemporary age, at all?

Our contemporary age

Without doubt, the age or epoch is one of our central temporal categories. The definition of the age stands in a position of transcendental observation of all events during a particular duration and established relations between them as the defining category of that age: Ancient Greece, the Enlightenment, Modernity. Indeed, it may strike the reader as odd that the age is not the category under consideration here. Surely an epoch sees more than a brothel? Ordinarily yes, but while the age can envelop so much, enveloping is the technical term for the least largest element that oversees a relation, there is nothing particular to the age that makes it 'larger' than the brothel. If in Genet's play or Badiou's reading the age can be seen from the position of the brothel, then the brothel envelops the age with differing semantic-functional effects. However, taking the age as the temporal category *par excellence*, there is nothing larger than the epoch except time itself, immediately one is struck by the ancient irresolution around epochs and ages which is that of Russell's paradox. How can you be a part of an age, say an important thinker of that age, and yet also take up a vantage point outside of that set of elements which compose the age, of which you are one, and define said age? As Badiou says, citing the poets, 'This means: contemporaneity itself is lacking. As if, between our thought and the present world, there was a gap . . . I would like to attempt to show this gap, to take the risk, if not of the present, at least of what separates us from it, which is of the order of representation, the order of the image' (PA 41). This I take to be the programme of the entire essay: what is it that separates us from our age, our present, our real? The answer he gives here couldn't be clearer, in a sense. Category theory is what separates us from being present in our world, for what else can it mean when he speaks of the 'order of representation', for that is just another way of saying the logics of appearing in worlds?

He goes on to speak of 'the ancient attempt to produce a real analysis of the images of the present age' (PA 41) which effectively provides us with several ages or several concepts of the age. We have the nature of our specific age as such, our contemporaneity within said age, the age-less nature of the order of representation, and an ancient discourse on the inability to produce the age. Thus, if we take the age as our first category, one that will later be subsumed as a diagram of our real category, brothel, it operates as a transcendental functor of a series of functional relations that all appear to share in common the dysfunction of temporal non-relation: the failure of images to capture the very thing they purport to represent, our now. If we take a world called temporality

then each age is made distinct and classified according to the
'rules' of that world, or 'conditions', as Badiou calls them. Time
is possessive of duration, segmentation, points, universality,
teleology, eschatology and so on, but an epoch of time has a
different structure. For example, in his study of epoch, *The
Century*, Badiou expresses a desire to define a century as a set of
categories and events contained within said century.[7] The seminar
upon which *The Century* is based pre-dates *Logiques*, but surely
this is a categorical rather than set-theoretical definition. If we
think of Modernity for a moment logically, the modern age is the
epochal category the book investigates, we can say that Modernity
is a concept that does or does not extend over objects. This
extensional position then equalizes the wealth of data that arises
intensionally when one studies, as I have done my entire adult
life, the cultural products of Modernity. The task of extensionally
is to take a diversity of information and say: these are all objects
of Modernity. The problem being that while extensional reasoning
works well in certain discourses of intense transmissible
communicability, empirical science, logic or maths, it fails to
encapsulate other areas, such as culture.

In addition, as Badiou says, what constitutes Modernity is,
well, what constitutes Modernity. There is no concept that extends
over objects, rather the creation of modern objects such as plays
combine to form a Modernity set. This is the axiom of separation
that defines sets as collections. Set theory has many abilities to

deal with this literal conceptual reversal, but the indifferential nature of multiples and their strict rankability does not make it a strong tool for large, messy systems.[8] Category theory, in contrast, is able to speak of a consistent age as being composed of whatever can be said to form a functional relation with said category without presupposing the category as a concept. It is not a concept, it is a functional overseer, a perspective, the least largest existential seal. Yet in this essay, at least, the age is not in the transcendental position. I cannot, for example, see the brothel from the age. If our epoch here is the contemporary,[9] *The Balcony* seems to sit outside of that age, on the fringes, in a prophetic, untimely state, neither modern nor postmodern, within the last century yet taken here to speak of the new. Plus the age, in the essay, is not the envelope of the objects included in the age at a categorical level. We cannot see, for example, the relation between pornography and the age except from the perspective of the play, proven by the fact that if we look at Badiou's definition of the age as democratic materialism in the preface to *Logics*, pornography is not visible from there.

The preface to *Logique des Mondes* is odd, to say the least. A long, rambling, at times fragmented consideration of what Badiou calls our 'age of democratic materialism'. In it, Badiou speaks directly of our age as being defined by the simple maxims there are bodies and there are languages.[10] Bodies convey the universal, biopolitical idea of our rights to life, but also of course the simple ontological necessity of being something rather than nothing. Languages, the so-called postmodern relativity of all our statements, that they are all equally true within their contexts, because their contexts as such, what he later calls their worlds, cannot be shown to be true, in that they are logical which means constructible. This is another way of saying that when multiples exist in worlds, due to their relations, the nature of these relations, even their possibility, is indifferent. Any thing can exist in any world by establishing some kind of relation with any other thing appearing in that world.

One of the strokes of genius of the book is the way Badiou appropriates this general definition, and maps it directly onto the mathematics of categories which concern themselves, in Badiou's reading anyway, with the formation of 'bodies' thanks to the relative, truthlessly constructed logics of the various worlds those bodies occupy. As this discussion progresses, Badiou then comes to the simple maxim not just of *Logiques* but his entire project, begun in 1982 with *Theory of the Subject*, defined in full with his 1988 work *Being and Event*, and concluded with the still massively overlooked *Logics of Worlds*. Put those three books together, accept the narrative of progression Badiou himself promulgates, and you come up with '*There are only bodies and languages, except that there are truths*'.[11] This is an important statement because of where it locates the event. He does not say, for example, there are only multiples and sets, except there are truths, or that there are situations and states, except there are truths. Rather, he says there are only bodies, diagrams, and languages, categories, except there are truths. Truths because events occur in worlds and worlds are definable in terms of their logics, which are described in *Logics of Worlds* as regards the mathematics of categories. There is, to put it bluntly, no mention of pornography here, no need for a phallus, no consideration of the image, when it comes to his thinking about our age. Or is that true, your honour? Let's look again at the exhibits presented to the court.

A category is an image

Badiou calls the order of representation, which we are naming the greater logic of worlds, the order of the image. He mentions an 'ancient attempt to produce a real analysis of the images of the present age', and in the same short paragraph 'a kind of description of the regime of images, insofar as they deliver us the times – or rather, don't deliver them' (PA 41). In some sense, then, the problematic of an age, an evental age which is also, by the time of Genet, a post- / pre-evental age, which Badiou wants to map onto another age, that of our contemporary epoch, to suggest the evental period, which is how he defines the age of the modern,[12] has some relational relevancy to our present period, the contemporary age as lacking, which Genet's play, what, predicts, illustrates, allegorizes? – has to be mapped onto a co-domain which is the regime of images. What is the regime of images? I put it to you, it is category theory.

A category is an image. Unlike a set, a category has to be diagrammatically consistent, which is why part of its logic is classical, and part intuitionist. These are, in effect, the two languages of all bodies which appear. Appearance, by the way, is a term from *Logiques*,[13] which Badiou uses in this short essay because Genet uses it when he is defining comedy as the appearance of the signified called the phallus. Badiou does point out that 'the most important word here is "appearing"' (PA 42), going on to accept the power of comedy and of theatre is the means by which it makes power appear in such a way as it is open to derision. For something to appear in a world, it must participate in a map or diagram of self-identity, and relation to other bodies. Here, then, is the classic diagram of a category which is, you may note, an image, not because it illustrates the logic of categories but because for a category to function, you have to be able to see the relations:

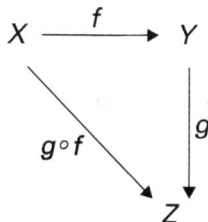

$$X \xrightarrow{\ f\ } Y$$
$$g \circ f \searrow \quad \downarrow g$$
$$Z$$

Not only is a category an image, it also defines a means of mapping anything onto anything else. Category theory as a whole is a meta-mathematical simplification of relations between objects which is structure-preserving no matter what category and network of relations you are talking about. It has no concern for the nature of the objects it describes, objects in category theory are even more radically indifferentiated than multiples in set theory, but only the functional direction of the relations between said objects shown here by the arrows or morphisms. In theory, therefore, if you wish to map two diverse objects onto the same space, what kinds of objects you choose is not directly relevant, rather how one acts on another and how both are acted on by a third is the crucial concern. This being the case there should be no reason why pornography (call it Y) cannot be mapped onto democracy (this would be Z) within a single category which we can call here 'brothel' (X in our diagram). What such a process achieves is the mapping of relational identities not in terms of ontological being, but rather the ontology of doing. If, for example, what democracy does with the image is functionally the same as what pornography does with the image, then democracy and pornography are the same, in terms of categories, even though, as I think I have shown, they have nothing in common in terms of what they are ontologically speaking.

Which leads us to a third way in which categories make themselves felt in the text. Categories are the ontology of action, specifically functional, directional, compossible, associative, dynamic, acts. In category theory what an object is, in a traditional sense, is irrelevant, it is what it does, specifically what it does to another object under the auspices of a third, the transcendental name of the category as a whole, that defines the essence of the category in terms of relational functions. This makes a categorical being explicit, extrinsic, exposed, perhaps exploitative.[14] A thing that acts on another thing in a manner for all to see. In this sense, one could argue that categories are 'pornographic' because they lay bare the functions of a world. In addition, like pornography, categories are defined by what they do, what they make happen, not by what they are or say. If a play is a good way of staging categories, then pornography, oddly, is another. There is nothing erotic about categories. Everything has to be there on show. Nor is there anything passive. Categories are about one object doing something to another. Categories can be dramatic, they can be risible, and they can be explicit, so yes they can be pornographic. Yet pornography, for all is applicability to a critique of our age, is not the category of the essay. For it to be so, it would have to possess a vantage point from which all the essay's diagrams are visible. This would include the brothel, the Chief of Police, and the phallus. These diagrams are not visible from the function $A \rightarrow P$, meaning that while pornography envelops democracy, something larger has to envelop it. Only the brothel possesses a balcony from which it can survey all the other diagrams; the brothel, therefore, is the category in this context.

Brothel as category

What does it mean to think of the brothel as category? To answer that, one has to think of the brothel as primarily empty of meaning. The category is just a vantage point, it has relations with all its diagrams, which means, overall, as a term it is semantically indifferent. For an object to have 'meaning' as a function, its relations with other objects have to be observable but the overall category as such is not observable because it is the observation *qua* observation function. In this way, it echoes the presentation *qua* presentation procedure of set theory and thus also maps perfectly onto Agamben's definition of the signature. A signature is an empty signifier that allows one to talk of statements and beings as if under the same heading, over time and across space. For example, the signature of Life itself has no referent, there is no centrally agreed upon thing which defines life. Even if this turns out to be ion cascades or quantum genetics, these will not 'explain' or 'define' the signatory power life has had for centuries, but just form a new archetype for Life as a signature.[15] Life, then, is also a category, under which objects of relations of force are organized, albeit in a much less formally structured way than in Badiou's work.

My point being that a category is devoid of meaning in that it facilitates all meaningful relations but is not included in them. In that sense, it is similar to the void in ontology, although it is also an actual infinity.[16] The transcendental is that which is not included in any world, such that the world as a non-whole can remain consistent. The category is the inexistent whole of any world as an actual infinity. This being the case, to define what brothel as category means, you actually need to ask what it does, or rather what it allows to happen underneath its auspices. The brothel as category is, on this reading, a structure of sanction and legitimization, allowing you to speak of things in the same breath, even if that breath as a whole may be beyond your comprehension. The definition of the brothel as category is the relational map of the diagrams it dominates. These are, within the article: our age, desire, phallic power, pornography, the image and democracy. All of these diagrams can be seen from the brothel, whereas no other diagram can see all these diagrams including the brothel. Thus the brothel is the category.

A category determines degrees of appearing of something relative to itself, another multiple, and a third multiple which can also be taken to be a transcendental function. It also maps appearing in a diagrammatic form which demands that every category is functionally stable by being presentable in a two-dimensional, tabular fashion: our triangular diagram. For any multiple to be in a world, it must appear in a world. Finally, every clump of diagrams, however disparate and distanced (categories are POSets) can be said to be in the same world if, from the vantage point of the transcendental of that world, they can be seen. My point, which I am reiterating here, is that a category is a logical theory of the image and of appearing. This being the case, it should not be controversial to call the brothel in Genet's play a category. The brothel determines the logic of appearing of the other diagrams we have mentioned, in terms of its functions of financial exploitation, visual explicitness, and of course sex.

Does Badiou say so? Not in so many terms, and yes this line of questioning might seem leading, but if your honour were to indulge me for a moment, when he says that Genet's play 'confronts the reign of images with the real of revolt' (PA 44), what else, members of the jury, can he mean? In miniature, this is a summation of *Logics of Worlds*. He then adds that there is a figure of order of images, a figure of order is a literal description of a categorical diagram, and that the name of that order is 'brothel'. A brothel is a strong example of a category because it is 'rigidly ordered', 'closed on its law' and 'governed entirely by the imaginary' (PA 44). Of the three, is it perhaps the third stipulation that is problematic? The Lacanian imaginary is not a category, surely? A category no, but a diagram of a category, absolutely. First, thanks to the mirror stage, the imaginary is formed out of a false imago or image. A child is able to see a reflected image of itself as already complete, already whole. This false image then becomes a dynamic driver of subjective desire, as the child and then adult tries to find images of itself to match this initial, complete self-image. What the imaginary says, simply, is that the world in question, here the world of subjectivity, is a whole, and that this wholeness is visible from an elevated vantage point, that of the mirror's reflection. This image is always a whole, even if, in truth, this was a prematurely complete imago, an imagined and visually presented quasi-whole. The aim of the subject ever after is to capture or re-imagine this foundational wholeness, a process that is impossible because that initial image's presentation of completion was a fraud, a trick of perspective, a false image. And because as a category this transcendental function of whole-making is by definition itself a non-whole. Finally, place the imaginary in relation to Lacan's ideas pertaining to the symbolic and the real, and time and again you see this represented as a triangulation of directional relations which are functions of one aspect, say the symbolic, on another, call it the real. And in this triangle, the imaginary is invariably located at the apex, the categorical position. In short, and this perhaps explains why Lacan features so strongly in the essay, Lacanian psychoanalysis is a theory of categories, meaning there is a direct relation in the essay between the imago, the imaginary and the category as image.

I hope you can see what there is in this formulation that Badiou can salvage for his logics of appearing. Like the imaginary in Lacan, a category is composed out of images of completion; we call this structure. They are false completions because every world is a one or coherent set of categories which is, however, not whole. In that category theory is about being able to see structure, and about making objects appear, it is in a sense like a mirror. The transcendental functor of a world reflects back, effectively, the overall coherence and structure of disparate parts as if they were whole. This is a kind of false image because every world behaves as if it were a one that is whole, but in that every world is an actual infinity, this is an operational fiction or mathematical imago. From this point on, every image of said world has to match that original, falsely complete imago.

Categorical functional fusion of pornography and democracy

We have proven that the brothel is a functional-preserving category whose function of relation Badiou determines as the fusion or total relation of 'the arousal of desire with the vulgarity of commercial propaganda. The brothel is the theatrical place of this fusion' (PA 44). This answers the question as to why Badiou wants to define our age as pornographic. Certainly, it conveys the cheapeningofourdemocracythankstorampantcommercialization, and the means by which democracy depends on images of desire, but as we said before, comparing two objects in a category is no challenge, what matters when you do so is what degree of intensity of appearing those two objects functionally hold with themselves when you compare them. However, the aim of the essay is, in my opinion, not predicative in its relations. It is not what qualities pornography and democracy share in common that is important here, categories can speak to this but only if they convert quality into a function, rather it is what functions they share in common; not what they are like but what they do and how this leads to their fusion. When two things fuse in categories, this does not signify that they become the same object, but that they have become subject to the same functional operation. Our question has to be, then, what fusion is, and how is it functionally possible between arousal of desire and commercial images, Badiou's stated aim in the morphism $P \rightarrow A$?

One of the greatest innovations of category theory is how it deals with identity, which is what I am taking fusion to mean. For example, within category theory, if two objects have the same intensity and order of relation to another object, then these two objects are identical because existence is defined by intensity of functional relation. If commercialization and the image were to fuse functionally, it could be because they both operate on the same objects in the same way, making the two objects the same.

Another mode of fusion concerns the value of commutativity. If you look again at our basic diagram of a category, you can see that all the arrows that start from X and end with Z travel in such a direction that if you start at X you will end up at Z whichever way you travel, meaning the value of $X \to Z$ is equal to $X \to Y \to Z$. This is what is meant by commutativity, and it shows that the functional relation between X and Z, has a direct relation to that from X, through Y, to Z. Commutative triangles define the logical completeness of any world by showing that 'the Relation between relations is itself the world' (LW 313). This is another kind of fusion. The fact that the brothel can occupy the position X in the commutative diagram that relates images to commercialization means this relation fuses into a world or category. The category brothel is the fusion of all the diagrams it can see into a world, which is another way of saying is conforms to the axiom of separation.

A third option is that due to the laws of compossible association, it matters which objects occupy which positions, leading to another sense of fusion. If the brothel oversees the commercialization of the image, then the diagram Brothel $\to$ Commercialization $\to$ Image is functionally tied to the diagram Brothel $\to$ Image. What this shows is that hidden in this simpler second function is the composite of the additional function. So that the brothel's exploitation of sexual arousal includes within it the role of commercialization. If you switch it around and say the direct function on the brothel to commercialization is the same as that from brothel to image to commercialization, you do not learn anything new about any element, meaning they are functionally fused: you can look at the functions in any order, as long as you keep to the law of association, and the result will always be the same. This is the meaning of commutativity, after all.

Triangles that have a degree of commutativity, when they are placed within the purviews of the universal terminal object or category, here brothel, are often then subject to what Badiou calls variously flattening or reduction,[17] especially when one is dealing with parallel functions as we are here. Between pornography and the age exist two functions, that of images of desire and that of commercialization. What we are actually enquiring after is how the category of the brothel allows us to see the double function that exists between pornography and age. Often, it will be the case in terms of parallel functions that one of the functional directions in a commutative triangle can be 'equalized' by the composite functions of another, meaning this line can be removed and the triangle flattened. Simplification of a diagram is similar to analysis in logic, and just as in logic you use analysis to move to the smallest possible equation, in category theory you are always looking for the least complex diagram. A flattened commutative diagram with two functions, which is what we are dealing with here, I think, looks like this:

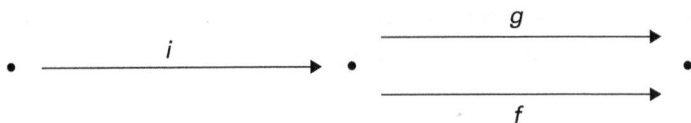

This is the diagrammatic presentation of identity in category theory. If the diagram were reversed and we had two lines becoming one, then this is called a monomorphism and is the diagrammatic presentation of difference.

If we think about the functional fusion Badiou is proposing, between images of desire and commercialization, what the diagram shows is that $f°i = g°i$, allowing us to flatten the two lines from X, the brothel as category, into one line, the composite associative line from X through Y to Z, because the line from X to Z is entirely determined by the composite line. This, then, is a final, composite fusion, that of the two functions when observed from a third position, we are calling this the brothel, or X, and that of the two lines of sight from the brothel to pornography and the age. Because of the law of association, the functional direction with the double function moves from pornography to the age. Thus the composite line of functional equivalence goes from brothel, through pornography, to the age. This means we can equalize or reduce the line from the brothel to the age, such that if we ever need to speak functionally of the age of democracy, we must speak of it through pornography. What this shows is that while pornography and the age are different objects, their functions are equalized, made the same, from the perspective of the brothel, which explains how commercialization and images of desire are equalized in the play. Another way of saying this is that the brothel as category functionally allows you to see how two very different things, pornography and the age, can be shown to be directly related, because their functional differences can be equalized from the perspective of the play, from its balcony of regard. To sum up, in terms of identity of relation, commutativity and finally equalization, for Badiou the brothel makes it visually possible, through staging, to present desire and capital as functionally the same, so that they fuse. And what is the name of the object of total relational intensity between sex and money, venerable members of the jury, why pornography of course!

We are finally able to concede the functional relation of our age, democratic materialism, to pornography due to identity of relation, identity of commutative function and, using parallel functions, identity of functional equalization. More than this, if we take the brothel to be our category, thanks to the staging of relations in Genet's play, we are able to map pornography onto the age in a manner that does not make them appear in the brothel with zero intensity, because of their functional fusion. The role of the brothel is not just to relate two diagrams, and the ambition of the essay cannot be to draw a diagram between pornography and our age, but rather to create a commutative image of their relation through the equalization of reduction of the parallel functions, commercialization and images of desire, such that when they appear in the brothel, you cannot tell them apart in terms of function. In this sense, the brothel is a mode of poeisis (poeisis is, after all, a function), of unveiling a truth of the identity of democratic materialism which is, diagrammatically speaking, that pornography and democracy are not analogous, similar, or even related, but that they are in fact, categorically speaking, functionally identical.

Power: the image of no image

For all the talk of a political Badiou, a fact not often remarked upon is that in his ontology or his objective phenomenology, there is no theory of power. Ontological order is not in place due to force, it is just ontological order. Similarly, if an object appears with more intensity because of another in a world, this is not necessarily to do with the power structures of that world. Like rankable order, sets of multiples, relational order, categories of diagrams, this is just the way things are.[18] Yet I have suggested that categories lend themselves to a theory of power that goes beyond political action for all of those, and we are surely the overwhelming majority, who think discourse, art, sexuality and the internet can all be political functions. Real political functions, not just those mocked in the essay as middle-class, intervallic navel-gazing, political load-bars while we wait for the App of the event to install.

For example, categorical objects act on each other due to a greater degree of intensity, for which read envelope of dominance. The envelope in category theory is, certainly, a theory of power bound by the useful stricture of the least largest. It tells us at the local, diagrammatic level, who is in charge functionally, who are their allies, who is central, who peripheral, and so on. While the category as a whole is a vantage point as surveillance as force, a powerfully Foucauldian idea wedded to remarkable formalism. A category therefore tells us how power really works. It is an image of the functions of the powers that be. Finally, the structural dialectic between categories, dominant power, and diagrams, local power, gives us a total portrait of the workings of constituting and constituted power, useful for oligarchs and Chavistas alike. *The Pornographic Age* is remarkable in Badiou's oeuvre, therefore, in the way in which the second half of the essay concerns how the denuding of the Chief of Police as phallic power in the play openly discusses what power is, how it operates and its relation to the image, aside from the call for evental revolution which the piece runs off into at the very end. If phallic power serves to sexualize power, it also allows us to see power, or rather to see the invisibility of power which, we learn from its control of the regimes of images, is its defining function. Which also perhaps answers the question as to why power does not feature more prominently in Badiou's work, namely because power cannot be imagined, imaged, drawn, or diagrammatically shown.

In a sense, Badiou names the overall challenge of the work as the 'relation or non-relation between the pure evental exteriority and the field of images, where the latent power of the event, the as-yet unrevealed sense of revolt, almost always comes to be lost in representation without thought' (PA 44). He may be talking about the real in the play, but he is certainly also considering his life-long commitment to the event, radically updated by category theory. For what he opines here is the manner in which events fail to be discerned in worlds due to the totalizing structuration of images that define categories. So that when he later asks 'can we subtract ourselves from images?' (PA 45), the question is pointed one. Are we able to emulate subtractive being in the field of images, categorical worlds, such that we can discern the indiscernible, or that which appears in a manner that is not imaged? Another means of describing the event. These are questions which make little or no sense from the pages of *Being and Event*, and let us know how the stakes have changed since its publication two decades ago.

One of the central problems of existence, categorically, is that something exists in a world only if it can be perceived from the vantage point of said category. In theory at least, anything which appears which cannot be seen by the categorical transcendental functor in actual fact does not appear in that world and so does not exist. The concomitant of this is that 'The image is the murder of the pure present ... The present of the present has no image. We must disimage, disimagine' (PA 46). As was the case with ontology, the event is impossible. In the logics of appearing, anything that can appear in a world is discernible, classified and relatable in a world such that the basic definition of the event as indiscernible, impossible to classify and non-relational precludes it from appearing in any world. Yet unlike ontology, Badiou clearly believes that the interdictions on the event are less absolute in terms of appearing as an impossible diagram in a category. If a multiple does not belong, then there is no such thing as said multiple. If a multiple, however, does not present itself to view, this does not negate said multiple, only its existence in this world. If we take the example of the Spartacus event, the multiple 'slave' comes to form a functional relation with 'free' which is literally indiscernible and non-communicable in Ancient Rome at the time.[19] It is not the multiple which is impossibly eventual, however, but its non-relational appearing in the world of Roman categories of citizenship and rights. No world can disallow any multiple from appearing in said world, giving the event a potentially infinite number of opportunities to appear in a designated world. That said, as soon as an event is perceptible to the transcendental functor, it is no longer, as he suggests here, an event. At the same time, every category is also a disciplinary actualization of the ban on all impossible relations. This is why events are rare, because categories are diagrammatically omniscient and censorious.

The function of disimaging, or disimagining, however, presents an interesting reversal of emphasis within the orthodox schema of the event. Traditionally Badiou presents us with a totally stable system, being or here worlds, and then shows how events can or cannot be seen to occur within those stabilities so as to destabilize them. In this essay, however, he speaks retroactively about the event as being stripped of its images, a unique alteration in Badiou's conceptual strategy in relation to fostering events. To disimage or disimagine seems quite the opposite to the process he calls enquiry in *Being and Event*, for example, which is pretty closely emulated in *Logics* as well, for that matter. In those books, events occur outside of ontology or logics of worlds, and are slowly made to appear by multiples being added to them, or related to them. Their compossibility, therefore, moves forward whereas here the disimaging process is surely running backwards. As if it is not so much that we need to find a way to see events, due to their circumstances, but reveal them by un-relating them from the images that negated their pure present-hood.

While this is intriguing, by his own admission it is also problematic. There is, he argues, something that itself is present in a world but which does not appear, emulating the ontological function of subtractive being. He names this naked power or power divested of its images such that you see it in full for the first time. Such a denuding of power is what the play appears to be about, but is a gesture much closer to Badiou's rival Agamben, surely. The real of power, like the real of the present, 'does not itself have an image' (PA 46), so that the event, for the first time, appears to have a rival. This is a new suggestion. In *Logics*, Badiou speaks of the reasons why events are intermittently rare, giving examples of different kinds of subjective positions that emerge from interaction with a singularity, reactive, obscure and faithful, only one of which becomes a true subject of the event.[20] He does not, however, mention that there is another possibility, which is that power may occupy the ontological position of subtraction and the evental condition of being without image, which in category theory means radically non-relational because relations are what diagrams realize imagistically. Power, then, pure naked power, masquerades as the event and as being, by taking off its mask and costume, bedazzling the senses with its lack of imagery. What can this mean categorically except that the transcendental functor is an imagistic shield for the power that keeps these functors in place as the controlling images of our world?

When, in the play at least, the phallic, denuded Chief of Police is made to appear as pure power as such, Badiou comments that 'we have the assembling of a structure. It's this structure that we can use to decipher the present age' (PA 49). It is a fascinating proposal for him. When power is revealed, in other words, its costume of occlusion is stripped away. Then, by definition, it forms a structure because being visible in relation is what a structure actually is. As it does so, and this is perhaps the key moment, this structure becomes a critical structure, a weapon against the age of the image. Turning the tools of categories against category is, of course, a more deconstructive gesture, just as denuding is a more Agambenian indifferential suspension. It appears to speak to alternative modes of powerful resistance within the system aside from the event.

We can now at least stipulate more clearly why Badiou is such an anti-democratic thinker. The problem with democracy is that of the image, which operates such that it 'covers with a false image naked power without image' (PA 50–1). Yet if democracy is about covering up the nudity of pure power, then surely it is not pornographic at all, but as I said censorious, and the idea of an age of pornography, making explicit the imagery of power as a commercial venture, is misplaced. It would appear on this reading that Badiou's critique, which lays bare the truth of power as being without image, is the more pornographic gesture. Either way, democracy, he argues, is a masking and clothing of power, so that categories themselves give a false sense of the transcendental functor as the basis of power. It occupies, after all, the godlike position we tend to equate with absolute power. What we learn instead is that the position of category is, primarily, a way of hiding power by suggesting force is determined by relation when, in truth, it is not. This is, to my knowledge, the first time Badiou has ever hinted at such a thing.

At the same time, there is something intrinsically powerful about images because, as he later explains, 'The key problem, for anyone who wants to escape the power of power, is to disengage from one's enchainments to images' (PA 52). Thus the structuration of the image, the category, may serve to mask power's lack of structuration, but if power is without structure, to escape from it you need not so much to deconstruct it as de-structure it for your own eyes, so to speak. You need to see power's lack of image-structure, it has to be staged for you. Could this be a completely new function of the event? Could it be that category theory is a mode of staging relationality and functions as the prime means for non-relational events because of this complex consideration of the relation/non-relation of power to its images? Certainly, one can say that the democratic age, which he defines as 'the consensual and pornographic image of market democracy' (PA ?), is defined as the manner in which a category, democracy, is placed in the position of transcendental functor, so that the myth of total visibility operates such that the truth of its actual power is hidden. Where better to hide power than nude, right in the middle of the agora of images, hidden in plain sight, as they say, like Poe's famous purloined letter?

It is the non-relational nature of pure power that means it cannot be seen, which is how it remains in total control of our entire existence. If the age of imagery is pornographic, then this is less to do with nudity than explicitness. Because we can see images, we simply cannot see the power behind them. This then gives us an opportunity to think the event one more time. There is a functional parity between event and power, is there not? Like power, the event cannot be seen, which means, as in the case of power, the event is not a structure. And if power is in truth structure-less, then the stultifying control that it has over every single image, due to its transcendentally functional proxies, can be relatively easily undermined by the event. Not, as Badiou has argued up to this point, due to the event's disruptive non-relationality becoming visible in a world, at which point like seriality its radical consequences will be lost, but rather because events as non-relational a-structural functions, reveal that power is also non-relational and a-structural. It is just that the event wants everyone, eventually, to see this, and power never does.

I know this is not what Badiou explicitly says of the event, but it could be over time taken to be what he means: events are not indiscernible elements that become discernible over time, but rather they are indiscernible critiques of power through step-by-step indiscernment of categories until finally, when all relation is lost, the non-relational, non-structural pure power itself is laid bare for all to see. This then suggests a special category, not a transcendental position from which all relations can be seen, and thus marketized and exploited (as is the case with big tech and our harvested data), but a categorical vantage point from which the non-necessity of relation is stripped bare. At this moment, the radical non-relationality of power and event is suddenly suspended, one can no longer tell the difference between revolution and the state, and when that happens, our age will surely come to a permanent close. If the event and power turn out to be functional parallels between categories and their enchained, because explicit, diagrams, then the equalization of the two functions is where real political power lies, in the identification of power and the event, such that yes, eventually, the event becomes visible and thus categorizable, but only if power is willing to draw a functional relation to it, for example by trying to negate it, such that power has to step out from behind the disguise of its categories, and stand before us nude and vulnerable.

For, after all, how can there be a pornography of democracy if everything is naked, everything made explicit, if the function of one thing on another is there for all to see, without titillation, without affect, and, most importantly of all, without shame? When that happens, the doors of the brothel will be flung open, and humanity will once again enter the paradise of the pure indifferentiation of gods, humans, police chiefs and prostitutes. Only then will we be truly naked, and only then will we finally be able to see power. This then is the message of the essay, and it is truly radical. Events function because of their functional parity with power, their non-relational invisibility. And the true wager of the event is that it can enter into a functional relation of parallelism with power, such that when the two are equalized, the event will regrettably be neutralized, but power will be visible and vulnerable, appearing on the balcony, visible to all, a clear target for the revolutionary crowd to draw a line of sight and establish a functional relation: fire! And so, members of the jury, I rest my case and await the court's judgement on my deposition.

NOTES

The Pornographic Age

1 S. Mallarmé, *Divigations*, 'Restricted Action', trans. Barbara Johnson (Harvard: Harvard University Press, 2009), p. 218.

2 A. Rimbaud, *A Season in Hell*, 'Deliria. Foolish Virgin. Hellish Husband', in *Rimbaud Complete*, trans. and ed. W. Mason (New York: Modern Library, 2003), p. 204. Translation modified.

3 J. Genet, *Le Balcon* (l'Arbalète, Décines, 1956). Badiou relies here on the first of Genet's three versions of this play, published in 1956. Although there is no official English translation of the first version, we have relied on Bernard Frechtman's revised 1966 version of Genet's 1963 revisions, *The Balcony* (New York: Grove Press, 1966). There are passages Badiou cites here that are not in the Frechtman translation; these we have restituted ourselves.

4 J. Lacan, *Formations of the Unconscious, Seminar V*.

5 J. Lacan, *Formations of the Unconscious, Seminar V*, p. 246.

6 Cf. A. Badiou, 'The Democratic Emblem', *Democracy in What State*, trans. W. McCuaig (New York: Columbia University Press, 2011), pp. 6–15, and 'A Speculative Disquisition on the Concept of Democracy', *Metapolitics*, pp. 78–95.

7 Cf. A. Badiou, *Logics of Worlds*, trans. A. Toscano (London: Continuum, 2007), p. 77.

8 This is our translation. To our knowledge, there is no extant translation of Genet's foreword.

9 Here, Badiou has recourse to the neologisms '*désimager*' and '*désimaginer*': the prefix '*dé*' (*dés*) in French has the general force of reversal, splitting, separation or dissemination.

10 Genet, *The Balcony*, p. 93.

11 Trans. modified.

12 Genet, *The Balcony*, pp. 77–8.

13 Genet, *The Balcony*, pp. 95–6.

14 H. Ibsen, *Emperor and Galilean: A World Historical Drama*, trans. B. Johnston (Lyme, NH: Smith and Kraus, 1999).

15 Ibsen, *Emperor and Galilean*, Part I, Act II, p. 36. Badiou appears to have modified Ibsen's line. All English translations of the play consulted render it: 'The old beauty is no longer beautiful and the new truth is no longer true.' Here is the line in Badiou's French: 'L'ancienne beauté n'est plus belle, et la nouvelle vérité n'est pas encore vraie.' See A. Badiou, *Pornographie du temps present* (Paris: Fayard, 2013), p. 43.

16 Genet, *Le Balcon,* Préface. Our translation.

Minus something indefinable

1 See, for example, A. J. Bartlett and J. Clemens, 'Translator's Foreword' in A. Badiou, *Happiness* (London: Bloomsbury, 2017), pp. 1–32.

2 Hence Jean Baudrillard will write: '*We no longer partake of the drama of alienation, but are in the ecstasy of communication.* And this ecstasy is obscene. Obscene is that which eliminates the gaze, the image and every representation. Obscenity is not confined to sexuality, because today there is a pornography of information and communication, a pornography of circuits and networks, of functions and objects in their legibility, availability', *The Ecstasy of Communication*, trans. B and S. Schutze (New York: Semiotext(e), 1988), p. 22; J.-F. Lyotard,

'Those who refuse to reexamine the rules of art pursue successful careers in mass conformism by communicating, by means of the "correct rules," the endemic desire for reality with objects and situations capable of gratifying it. Pornography is the use of photography and film to such an end. It is becoming a general model for the visual or narrative arts which have not met the challenge of the mass media', *The Postmodern Condition*, trans. G. Bennington and B. Massumi, with intro. F. Jameson (Manchester: Manchester University Press, 1984), p. 75. But one could just as easily cite the work of Giorgio Agamben, Roland Barthes, Michel Foucault, Gayle Rubin, Susan Sontag, and many others, for whom the thinking of pornography is a crucial task for our times.

3 Ian Hunter, David Saunders and Dugald Williamson, *On Pornography: Literature, Sexuality and Obscenity Law* (London: Macmillan, 1993), p. 229.

4 Lynn Hunt (ed.), *The Invention of Pornography: Obscenity and the Origins of Modernity, 1500–1800* (New York: Zone, 1993), p. 13.

5 Hunt, p. 23. Regarding the relationships between pornography and feminism, see the extraordinary book by Frances Ferguson, whose provocative title is supplemented by a subtitle which gives the sense of the argument: *Pornography the Theory: What Utilitarianism Did to Action* (Chicago: University of Chicago Press, 2004). This question has obviously been crucial in the history and development of second-wave feminism, for which the work of Andrea Dworkin, Catherine A. MacKinnon and Robin Morgan, among many others, has been definitive. See, for instance, Catherine A. MacKinnon, *Feminism Unmodified: Discourses on Life and Law* (Cambridge, Mass.: Harvard University Press, 1987) and Robin Morgan, 'Theory and Practice: Pornography and Rape', in *Take Back the Night*, ed. Laura Lederer (New York: William Morrow, 1980).

6 J. Murphet, 'Rosa Plus Emma: Political Pleasure and the Enjoyment of Reason', *Filozofski vestnik*, Vol. XXXVI, No. 2 (2016), p. 202.

7 A. Badiou and N. Truong, *In Praise of Theatre*, trans. with intro. A. Bielski (London: Polity, 2015), p. 1.

8 A. Badiou, *Ahmed the Philosopher: Thirty-Four Short Plays for Children and Everyone Else*, trans. J. Litvak (New York: Columbia University Press, 2014). In the Preface to the English edition Badiou notes that in comedic theatre 'the hero is usually a representative of the lowest class. Comedy reveals the world of the rich and the powerful from the violent, ironic, and critical perspective of the oppressed and the poor. The hero of Plautus's Latin plays is always a slave, that of Molière's comedies a valet. My hero would be Ahmed, the immigrant worker of our housing projects' (p. vii). Badiou also notes that he created the character to counter the insidious attacks against immigrant workers in France: this situational political reference should be kept in mind throughout.

9 O. Feltham, 'Biography and Early Works', *Badiou: Key Concepts*, ed. A. J. Bartlett and J. Clemens (Durham: Acumen, 2010), p. 10.

10 Badiou and Truong, *In Praise of Theatre*, p. 1.

11 Badiou and Truong, *In Praise of Theatre*, p. 3.

12 A. Badiou, *Rhapsody for the Theatre*, trans. B. Bosteels, *Theatre Survey*, Vol. 49, No. 2 (November 2008), p. 189.

13 This volume, p. 2.

14 A. Badiou, *Manifesto for Philosophy*, trans. Norman Maderasz (Albany: SUNY Press, 1999). As Badiou explains in an interview: 'You know, my philosophical history is in some sense a strange history of a relationship to Plato. Because at the very beginning of my philosophical life I was a Sartrean! And to be a Sartrean was to be against Plato. No problem, because existence is what is important not essence. But another part of myself was on the side of Plato.' 'Mathematics', 'The Movement of Emancipation', 'Round Table Interview with Alain Badiou', *Badiou and His Interlocutors: Lectures, Interviews and Responses*, ed. A. J. Bartlett and J. Clemens (London: Bloomsbury, 2017).

15 A. Badiou, *Rhapsody for the Theatre*, p. 207.

16 See Lacan referring to the personages of *The Balcony*: 'Each of these characters represents functions from which the subject finds himself alienated – they are functions of speech of which he finds himself the support but which go well beyond his singularity', J. Lacan, *Formations of the Unconscious, Book V*, ed. Jacques-Alain Miller, trans. Russell Grigg (Cambridge: Polity, 2017), p. 247. Thanks to Russell Grigg for an early look at the manuscript.

17 See Plato, *The Apology*, where Socrates' trial for impiety and the corruption of youth turns on the testimony of Meletus, aggrieved on behalf of the poets; Anytus, the professional men and politicians; and Lycon, the orators (Ap. 23e). These three *formalize* the charges made against Socrates his whole life. For Plato, all share the same knowledge of what knowledge must be. Of this, Socrates knows nothing and so, finally, must not be. In *Complete Works*, ed. John M. Cooper and D. S. Hutchinson (Indianapolis: Hackett Publishing, 1997).

18 See the early lines of the very first dialogue, *The Apology* (Ap. 17a–c), where Socrates distinguishes his relation to words from those of the 'orator'. This is *the* stage direction, as it were, for the entirety of the dialogues of Plato.

19 For a full typology of these encounters, see A. J. Bartlett, *Badiou and Plato: An Education by Truths* (Edinburgh: Edinburgh University Press, 2011/15), pp. 155–60.

20 On this turn, and the ubiquity of it being understood thus, see Bartlett, *Badiou and Plato*, pp. 180–91.

21 More specifically: 'Comedy embraces, gathers and takes enjoyment from the relationship with an effect that has a fundamental relation to the signifying order, namely the appearance of this signified called the phallus.' J. Lacan, *Formations of the Unconscious*, p. 246.

22 H. J. Rose, *Handbook of Greek Literature: From Homer to the Age of Lucien* (London: Methuen, 1950), p. 214.

23 J. Genet, *The Balcony*, trans. Bernard Frechtman (New York: Grove Press, 1966), p. 50.

24 'But all true Theatre is a heresy in action. I have the habit of calling its orthodoxy "theatre": an innocent and prosperous ritual, from which

Theatre detaches itself as a rather implausible lightning bolt.'
A. Badiou, *Rhapsody for the Theatre*, p. 187.

25　A. Badiou, 'A Speculative Disquisition on the Concept of Democracy',
Metapolitcs, trans. J. Barker (London: Verso, 2005), p. 78.

26　Genet, *The Balcony*, p. 36.

27　This volume, p. 19.

28　Badiou, 'Speculative Disquisition', p. 78.

29　Badiou, *Rhapsody for the Theatre*, pp. 187–8. Badiou is referring here to
François Regnault's work, *The Spectator*, 'which is a nearly complete
treatise on modern theatre'.

30　Against, then, the contemporary double bind of the fetish for
turning the theatre of the Cave into a putative cinema *and* also
against the conflation of the two, we choose here to see the Cave as
Theatre, while taking on Badiou's analysis of the disjunction at the
heart of the knowledge of theatre itself, split between the theatre
of the State and the truth of Theatre. For a study of Badiou and
cinema whose veracity stands the test of this disjunction in terms
of 'the passage of the idea', which it doesn't fail to see, see A. Ling,
Badiou and Cinema (Edinburgh: Edinburgh University Press,
2010).

31　Plato, *Republic*, trans. G. M. A. Grube, rev. C. D. C. Reeve, *Complete
Works*, pp. 971–1223, 515c.

32　Badiou, *Rhapsody for the Theatre*, p. 193.

33　Badiou, *Rhapsody for the Theatre*, p. 193. Badiou distinguishes between
Theatre (with a capital) and theatre, similar to the way he distinguishes
'politics' and 'the political' in *Metapolitcs*, see p. 187.

34　Lacan notes: 'It is the eternal problem in this whole story to know how
Aristophanes, the comic poet, found himself there with Socrates,
whom as everyone knows he did more than criticize, whom he
ridiculed, defamed in his comedies and who, generally speaking,
historians hold in part responsible for the tragic end of Socrates,
namely his condemnation.' J. Lacan, *Transference, Seminar VIII*, trans.

Cormack Gallagher, 30.11.60 III 36. Cf. 'When Pausanias finally came
to a pause (I've learned this sort of fine figure from our clever
rhetoricians), it was Aristophanes' turn, according to Aristodemus.
But he had such a bad case of the hiccups – he'd probably stuffed
himself again, though, of course, it could have been anything – that
making a speech was totally out of the question.' Plato, *Symposium*,
(185c), trans. Alexander Nehamas and Paul Woodruff, *Complete Works*,
pp. 457–505.

35 In Plato's dialogues, the medical man is not a respected figure, his
biological empiricism, so to speak, leaves too much to be desired and
his appearance as a man of status is the symptom of a more profound
lack.

36 J. Lacan, *Transference, Seminar VIII*, 14.12.60 V 68.

37 Apropos: 'And so he lives on, yielding day by day to the desire at hand.
Sometimes he drinks heavily while listening to the flute; at other times,
he drinks only water and is on a diet; sometimes he goes in for
physical training; [d] at other times, he's idle and neglects everything;
and sometimes he even occupies himself with what he takes to be
philosophy. He often engages in politics, leaping up from his seat and
saying and doing whatever comes into his mind. If he happens to
admire soldiers, he's carried in that direction, if money-makers, in that
one. There's neither order nor necessity in his life, but he calls it
pleasant, free, and blessedly happy, and he follows it for as long as he
lives . . . I also suppose that he's a complex man, full of all sorts of
characters, fine and multi-coloured . . .' Out of this (and more), Plato
then argues, naturally comes tyranny. The Republic is the effort to
thwart nature by thought. See Plato, *The Republic*, 561d, *Complete
Works*, p. 1172.

38 Plato, *The Republic*, 557d: 'So it looks as though anyone who wants to
put a city in order, as we were doing, should probably go to a
democracy, as to a supermarket of constitutions, pick out whatever
pleases him, and establish that', *Complete Works*, p. 1168.

39 Moreover, Theatre and Cinema produce a distinct 'audience': 'if
cinema is everywhere, it is no doubt because it requires no spectator,

only the walls surrounding a viewing public. Let's say that a spectator is real, whereas a viewing public is merely a reality, the lack of which is as full as a full house, since it is only a matter of counting. Cinema counts the viewers, whereas Theatre counts on the spectator . . ', and 'cinema, unlike theatre, is by no means a public place, even if it appears to be one. What is wrapped in obscurity is the private individual . . ', Badiou, *Rhapsody for the Theatre*, pp. 187–8.

40 J. Baudrillard, 'Simulacra and Simulations', in *Jean Baudrillard: Selected Writings*, trans. Paul Foss, Paul Patton and Philip Beitchman, ed. Mark Poster (Stanford: Stanford University Press, 1988), pp. 171–2. We have swapped out Disneyland for Hollywood here, and of course we have not gone all the way with Baudrillard toward the simulation of the real, but the analysis of the way appearance functions to effect the displacement of the real as a true fiction is apropos: Los Angeles is encircled by these 'imaginary stations' which feed reality, reality-energy, to a town whose mystery is precisely that it is nothing more than a network of endless, unreal circulation: a town of fabulous proportions, but without space or dimensions. As much as electrical and nuclear power stations, as much as film studios, this town, which is nothing more than an immense script and a perpetual motion picture, needs this old imaginary made up of childhood signals and faked phantasms for its sympathetic nervous system.

41 Genet, *The Balcony*, p. 41.

42 Genet, *The Balcony*, pp. 93–4.

43 Genet, *The Balcony*, p. 48.

44 'Mallarmé claims that in his time (but ours is worth as little as his) there is nothing historically real, for lack of a self-declared political collective, and, consequently, that it is theatre that gathers whatever is available to us in terms of action', Badiou, *Rhapsody for the Theatre*, p. 189.

45 Badiou, *Rhapsody for the Theatre,* p. 232.

46 Lacan, *Formations of the Unconscious*, p. 260.

47 See Badiou, *Rhapsody for the Theatre*, p. 194.

48 A. Badiou, *Handbook of Inaesthetics*, trans. A. Toscano (Stanford: Stanford University Press, 2004), p. 17.

49 Badiou, *Handbook of Inaesthetics,* p. 18.

50 In the essay 'The Return of Philosophy to Itself', Badiou laments that in Book X of *Laws* Plato has himself seemingly abandoned this aporetic opening of thought to the thinking of the new in favour of the rule and the law. See A. Badiou, *Manifesto for Philosophy*, trans. Norman Maderasz (Albany: SUNY Press, 1999), p. 122. In *Badiou and Plato: And Education by Truths*, Bartlett argues against this charge of Badiou, noting: 'suffice to say that th[is] argument of the *Laws* is directed explicitly against the sophistic tendency which dissembles in support of whatever contemporary interests are at stake, and the summary prescriptions against impiety and corruption are entirely consistent with Socrates' public position in the *Apology*, to wit "the gods exist, they are concerned with us, and they are absolutely above being corrupted into flouting justice"' (L. 907b). The position of Socrates in the *Apology*, and Plato across the entire corpus, is that in regard to all these things it is only Socrates, thus, the *figure of Socrates*, who would speak the truth (Ap. 17a). These 'criminal laws', as Badiou calls them, are the rational result of a thinking directed towards ensuring the continued failure of the corruptions of sophistry. Quite simply, and this is the non-dialectical inversion staged by Plato, to corrupt the corrupt is the work of reason, while to corrupt the work of reason is corrupt, pp. 346–7.

51 'Plato must himself resort to images, like that of the sun; to metaphors, like those of 'prestige' or 'power'; to myths, like the myth of Er the Pamphylian returning to the kingdom of the dead. In short, when what is at stake is the opening of thought to the principle of the thinkable, when thought must be absorbed in the grasp of what establishes it as thought, we witness Plato himself submitting language to the power of poetic speech', Badiou, *Handbook of Inaesthetics,* pp. 19–20. Elsewhere, Badiou will attribute this retreat to images as an effect of the limits of the mathematics available to Plato to think this principle of thought otherwise.

52 A. Badiou, *Theory of the Subject*, trans. B. Bosteels (London:
        Continuum, 2009), p. 184. For Badiou's discussion of the development
        of his relation to Plato, see 'The Movement of Emancipation', Round
        Table Interview with Alain Badiou, in *Badiou and His Interlocutors:
        Lectures, Interviews and Responses*, pp. 219–35.

53 Badiou, *Manifesto for Philosophy*, pp. 97–109. For the full elaboration
        of this ontology of the multiple and the subject of truths one cannot
        avoid or fake working through *Being and Event*.

54 A. Badiou, *Theoretical Writings*, ed. and trans. R. Brassier and
        A. Toscano (London: Continuum, 2004), p. 37.

55 A. Badiou, *Logics of Worlds*, trans. A. Toscano (London: Continuum,
        2007), p. 511.

56 A. Badiou, *Being and Event*, trans. O. Feltham (London: Continuum,
        2005), p. 435. See Badiou, *Logics of Worlds*, p. 510.

57 'Plato's dialogues are and were in Plato's lifetime occasions to
        philosophize further, not dogmatic treatises', Debra Nails, *Agora,
        Academy and the Conduct of Philosophy* (Dordrecht: Kluwer Academic
        Publishers, 1995), p. 4.

58 Badiou, *Logics of Worlds*, p. 514.

59 Badiou, *Being and Event*, p. 58.

60 A. Badiou and T. Tho, 'The Concept of Model, Forty Years Later: An
        Interview with Alain Badiou', *The Concept of Model*, p. 92.

61 Badiou, *The Concept of Model*, p. 92.

62 Badiou, *Being and Event*, p. 56.

63 Badiou, *Theoretical Writings*, p. 49.

64 Badiou, *Logics of Worlds*, pp. 301–2.

65 See Badiou, *Being and Event*, p. 37; *Theoretical Writings*, pp. 151–2.

66 Badiou is considering the theatre as that which from out of its
        disparate parts – script, actors, scenes, stage, etc. – is an assemblage
        which in its act produces ideas. These ideas are producible nowhere

else and thus are theatre ideas: 'The idea arises in and by the performance, through the act of theatrical representation. The idea is irreducibly theatrical and does not pre-exist before its arrival on stage.' If, as Badiou contends, philosophy thinks the thought of theatre, then Plato's rivalry with theatre is nevertheless an effort to theatricalize the Idea in a way which transcends the specificities of its construction without for all that negating them as the necessary condition of this transcendence. The sensible as intelligible.

67 Plato, *The Republic* (518cd), *Complete Works*, pp. 1135–6.

68 Badiou, *Logics of Worlds*, p. 514.

69 Badiou, *Handbook of Inaesthetics*, p. 77.

70 Badiou, *Handbook of Inaesthetics*, p. 76.

71 '[Philosophy's] particular function is to arrange multiples for a random encounter with such a procedure. However, whether such an encounter takes place, and whether the multiples thus arranged turn out to be connected to the supernumerary name of the event, does not depend upon philosophy. A philosophy worthy of the name – the name which began with Parmenides – is in any case antinomical to the service of goods, inasmuch as it endeavours to be at the service of truths; one can always endeavour to be at the service of something that one does not constitute. . . . In any case, there is no commercial philosophy.' Badiou, *Being and Event*, p. 341.

72 A. Badiou and B. Bosteels, 'Can Change Be Thought: A Dialogue with Alain Badiou', *Alain Badiou: Philosophy and its Conditions*, ed. Gabriel Riera (New York: SUNY Press, 2005), pp. 252–3.

73 Plato, *Cratylus* (428d), trans. C. D. C Reeve, in *Complete Works*, pp. 101–56.

74 In the *Theaetetus*, Homer and Heraclitus are linked with Protagoras in that they have converged into the single idea that knowledge is perception, Plato, *Theaetetus*, 160d–e, pp. 404–5. In the *Cratylus*, Plato links Heraclitus to both Homer and Hesiod: 'everything gives way, nothing stands fast', Plato, *Cratylus* (402bcd), pp. 289–90.

75 See Lacan's description of the characters of *The Balcony*: 'the power
    that Christ confers on the posterity of Saint Peter and all episcopacies
    to bind and unbind the order of sin and transgression; the power of
    the person who condemns and punishes, namely the judge; the power
    of the person who assumes command in this great phenomenon, war,
    the power of the warlord, more typically the general. Each of these
    characters represents functions from which the subject finds himself
    alienated – they are functions of speech of which he finds himself the
    support but which go well beyond his singularity', *Formations of the
    Unconscious*, p. 247.

76 Badiou, *Being and Event*, p. 37. See also A. Badiou, *Parménide: L'être I
    – Figure ontologique 1985–1986* (Paris: Fayard, 2014).

77 Badiou, *Being and Event*, p. 34.

78 Plato, *Theaetetus* (152e and 167a), pp. 169–70, p. 185.

79 These are: the vitalist (Nietzsche, Bergson, Deleuze); the analytic
    (Russell, Wittgenstein, Carnap); the Marxist; the existentialist
    (Kierkegaard, Sartre); the Heideggerian; and the 'political philosophers'
    (Arendt and Popper).

80 A. Badiou, *Infinite Thought*, trans. J. Clemens and O. Feltham (London:
    Continuum, 2003), p. 46.

81 Badiou, *Infinite Thought*, p. 46.

82 Badiou, *Manifesto for Philosophy*, p. 85.

83 A. Badiou, *Deleuze: The Clamor of Being*, trans. L. Burchill (Minnesota:
    University of Minnesota Press, 2000), p. 102.

84 A. Badiou, *Manifesto for Philosophy* (trans. modified), p. 133. See
    Barbara Cassin, 'Who's Afraid of the Sophists? Against Ethical
    Correctness', trans. Charles T. Wolfe, *Hypatia*, Vol. 15, no. 4 (2000),
    pp. 116–17.

85 Badiou, *Infinite Thought*, p. 47.

86 Badiou, *Theoretical Writings*, p. 30.

87 Badiou, *Theoretical Writings*, pp. 47–8.

88 Badiou, *Handbook of Inaesthetics*, p. 76.

89 Badiou, *Handbook of Inaesthetics*, p. 27.

90 Badiou, *Theoretical Writings*, p. 31.

91 Badiou, *Handbook of Inaesthetics*, p. 72.

92 Badiou, *Handbook of Inaesthetics*, p. 73.

93 Badiou, *Handbook of Inaesthetics*, p. 75.

94 Badiou is citing the great French director Antoine Vitez, *Handbook of Inaesthetics*, p. 72.

Brothel as category

1 Alain Badiou, *Logics of Worlds*, trans. Alberto Toscano (London: Continuum, 2009), pp. 116–18.

2 *Logics of Worlds*, pp. 211–16.

3 Ibid., pp. 79–90.

4 I exclude any comments here in relation to the recently published third volume of the project, *L'immenance des vérités*.

5 Alain Badiou, *Mathematics of the Transcendental*, trans. A. J. Bartlett and Alex Ling (London: Bloomsbury, 2014), pp. 21–5.

6 This is conveyed in *Logics* by the basic relational function: ≥.

7 Alain Badiou, *The Century*, trans. Alberto Toscano (Cambridge: Polity, 2007), p. 3.

8 The thesis that Badiou's ontology is determined by the indifferential nature of multiples and of being is expressed in William Watkin, *Badiou and Indifferent Being* (London: Bloomsbury, 2017).

9 There is a great deal more to be said about Badiou's engagement with this term than we have space for here. For more on this topic, see

William Watkin, 'Mandelstam's Age, Badiou's Event, and Agamben's Contemporary', *CounterText* (2.1) 2016: 85–99.

10 *Logics of Worlds*, p. 1.

11 Ibid., p. 4.

12 Watkin, 'Mandelstam's Age', p. 87.

13 Book II, Section 1 of *Logics of Worlds* concerns itself with the logics of appearing.

14 *Mathematics of the Transcendental*, p. 15.

15 See Giorgio Agamben, *The Signature of All Things: On Method*, trans. Luca D'Isanto and Kevin Attell (New York: Zone Books, 2009), pp. 33–80, and William Watkin, *Agamben and Indifferent Being* (London: Rowman & Littlefield International, 2014), pp. 18–23.

16 See *Mathematics of the Transcendental,* pp. 15–16, on the complex issue of categories and infinity.

17 *Mathematics of the Transcendental*, pp. 31–2.

18 Without getting into the complexity of this, Badiou's point is that both set and category theory are based on a materialism which means they are not just constructible systems but systems constructed out of a relationship with the void as real. Most would be aware of this insistence when it comes to multiples, but for the doubters among you, consider the evidence placed before you in *Logics of Worlds*, p. 4.

19 *Logics of Worlds*, pp. 50–4.

20 *Logics of Worlds*, p. 62.